René Albrecht-Carrié is an authority on the history of the modern world. He is Professor of History and Chairman of the Department at Barnard College of Columbia University. Among his published works are *Italy from Napoleon to Mussolini*; *A Diplomatic History of Europe Since the Congress of Vienna*; *France, Europe, and the Two World Wars*; *Europe Since 1815*; and *One Europe: The Historical Background of European Unity*.

The
Meaning
of the
First World War

René Albrecht-Carrié

A SPECTRUM BOOK
Prentice-Hall, Inc.
Englewood Cliffs, New Jersey

To those who died,

thinking it not in vain

Current printing (last digit):

14   13   12   11   10   9   8   7

Preface

When, fifty years ago, in June, some youthful South Slav enthusiasts in the small Balkan town of Sarajevo assassinated the heir to the ancient Habsburg crown, little could they have foreseen the far-reaching repercussions of their deed. The passage of half a century seems an appropriate time to reappraise an event that can be viewed in more adequate perspective, and a currently flourishing literature bears witness to the revival of interest in the First World War.

Fifty years means two generations, and the youth of today tends to view the 1914 war as belonging to the historic past, much as the wars of Napoleon do. That youth is also taught to regard the First World War as one of the important turning points in history. In a sense the very phrase *turning point* is a misnomer when applied to historic development, which is characterized instead by continuity; the present is always the fruition of the seeds contained in the past, while itself already pregnant with the future. Yet in another sense the phrase is warranted. For if development has continuity and change is steadily occurring, the rhythm of such change nevertheless varies. Much has been written, for example, about the origins and the background of the French Revolution, yet that event itself stands out. The same is true of the First World War. Accumulated tensions, unresolved problems, will on occasion burst the mold of established institutions and erupt through the seemingly tranquil surface of deceptive stability.

It is the purpose of the present essay to explain precisely in what sense and what manner the 1914 war constitutes such a break with the past. To Americans this thesis may seem open to question, and they may feel inclined to place greater stress on such events as the Great Depression, or the Second World War with its consequent advent of the nuclear age. But, taking a larger world view, the greater emphasis belongs on the earlier occurrence.

v

One development that sums up many others may be described as the passing of the European Age. During the relative stability characteristic of the nineteenth century, Europe achieved—or perhaps better, completed—the conquest of the planet. This must of course be understood in a very broad sense, for although Europe asserted control of much of the world in the crude form of power, more importance attaches to the transference to the rest of the world of institutions, ideas, and ways whose home was European. In this context, imperialism in the narrow sense dwindles into a passage, one that contains the seeds of its own termination. The age of European dominance nevertheless is an important phase.

The rise to primacy of America, the emergence of the dependent peoples, the establishment of the Marxist ideology in Russia, are all developments which may properly be credited to the First World War, even though some of them did not achieve full recognition or success until the Second. That conflict was in fact but an extension of the earlier one, the unfinished task of which in many respects it merely completed.

From this interpretation it naturally follows that our attention should be focused on Europe. In addition, since most of the developments of the last half-century, however seemingly unexpected or surprising, have their roots in the past, it is necessary to understand the main currents of that past. The bases of American power lay in the nineteenth-century growth of America, and Marx is likewise a nineteenth-century figure. For that reason it has been thought desirable to explain "The Setting" of 1914 in the first part of this essay.

Then came the war—unexpected, unwanted, yet quite logical in the sense that it was the expression of the failure to resolve the problems and the tensions of the preceding era. War is itself a great promoter of change, and the course of it often strewn with or distorted by unforeseen accident. No one, among the initial belligerents, looked to a fundamental alteration in the shape of Europe; they all predicted a very short war. The duration and the course of the conflict belied all expectations, and the almost simultaneous outbreak of revolution in Russia and intervention by the United States combined to change radically the nature and the issues of the war. Yet all of these events may be traced to trends long existing. This is discussed in the main part of the essay, "The Performance," which examines the war and the subsequent peace, or perhaps we should say the attempted peace.

"The Meaning" lies in the fact that the magnitude of the break, or the acceleration of the rate of change, was such as to prevent any lasting solution. We are still in the midst of a period of transition, and, in the reckoning, our century may appear to bear considerable resemblance to that other era of transition, the sixteenth. For that reason it has been necessary to examine developments that extend over the period sometimes referred to as the second Thirty Years War.

Finally, it will appear that the whole essay gives a large place to the role of international affairs. This is intentional, for if One World still belongs in the domain of Utopia, in another sense we have such a world. No better illustration of this may be cited than the degree to which the United States, by force of circumstances rather than by deliberate choice, finds itself now involved in a network of world-encompassing commitments. Technological progress alone would suffice to account for such a situation, and there hardly seems need to emphasize the extent to which occurrences in one part of the world have repercussions in others. It is certainly significant that incidents of small dimensions in themselves, as those associated with the names of Sarajevo or Danzig, should have been the starting points of conflicts that became two world wars. We are now well aware that distant local happenings in Laos or the Congo, to take but random examples, contain similar dangers. The inauguration of such a state of affairs, the growing consciousness of world interdependence above all, may well be credited to the First World War. In this lies much of its significance.

R. A-C.

The author wishes to thank the Oxford University Press for permission to use the maps on pages 53 and 108, from *The War in Maps* by Francis Brown (copyright 1946 by Oxford University Press, Inc.).

Contents

ix

I

The Setting

Europe and the World in 1914

The nineteenth century is now often regarded as a century of peace, a view certainly warranted by the contrast between it and our own time of cataclysmic strife. That era sharply came to an end in 1914. The pace of change thereafter, the magnitude and the intensity of struggle, have been characteristic of the twentieth century transition, still in process of seeking an elusive stability.

Since the theme of this essay is the significance of the break that 1914 initiated, a brief glance at the world of 1914 is a necessary introduction, the better to bring out in full the measure of contrast. A general knowledge of the antecedents of that world, mainly the course of nineteenth-century developments, is assumed on the part of the reader; no more will therefore be attempted in this opening section than a brief sketch designed to bring into sharper relief and clearer proportion the main features of the 1914 canvas. In doing this the focus will in large measure be on Europe, which is warranted by two considerations: first, the degree to which Europe meant the whole world, owing to the controlling influence that Europe exercised over the major part of the planet; second, the simple fact that the First World War was unquestionably European in its origins, and that as a logical consequence it was fought out and settled primarily in Europe.

1

The Deep Forces of Change before 1914

We hear much at the present time about the population explosion. Concern is expressed over the consequences of that phenomenon, which remind one of the gloomy forecasts already voiced by Malthus in Napoleon's time. But there was little discussion of that issue before 1914 for the simple reason that the nineteenth-century record seemed to belie the seriousness of such predictions. Not only did Europe during that interval send more than fifty million of her sons to people the far and empty corners of the world, but her own resident population roughly trebled, while its standard of living was generally rising.

The increase, to be sure, was uneven and did in fact result in certain pressures. There was much land in Russia, but Italy was becoming crowded, though one must bear in mind that over- and underpopulation are relative terms which have little significance save in connection with the standard of living. That standard was indeed low for many, but the old, primitive curse of famine was largely a thing of the past. With the marked exception of France,[1] substantial and rapid growth was the rule everywhere. But it is also well to point out that one important nineteenth-century condition, the existence of vast empty spaces in many parts of the planet, was a passing circumstance, hence that the seeds of some later problems were already germinating. Malthus is now honored again.

In broad terms, the answer to the question of how increasing numbers could enjoy greater amenities lies in the one word, *ma-*

[1] The marked increase in numbers was mainly due to a sharp fall in the death rate, a result of the introduction of elementary sanitary measures and of improved medical knowledge.

At the beginning of the century France was still the most populous state of Europe, barring Russia. But the decline of her birth rate lost her that position. By the time of the Franco-Prussian War the French population had reached virtual stability while others continued thereafter to grow at an appreciable rate.

chine—or better industry. The old view that the totality of resources was limited and constant had long ago been destroyed by the incontrovertible fact that industry is a creator of wealth. The phenomenon called the Industrial Revolution is usually considered to have had its origin in England. Certainly it gave the island kingdom a position of economic primacy, but it could hardly be expected that Britain would forever remain the exclusive workshop of the world. Thus the nineteenth century witnessed the spread of industry from its initial British home, across the Channel first, into Belgium and northern France, then in an ever broadening wave that spread east and southeast. In this also growth was uneven. By the time of the Franco-Prussian War France and the future Germany had reached a roughly similar stage of development, but thereafter, owing partly to the stimulus of unification, Germany forged ahead by leaps and bounds, far outdistancing France, as she did also in numbers, and even challenging the primacy of Britain, whose steel production her own had passed before 1914. As the present century opened, one could already make an appropriate distinction between "inner" and "outer" Europe. The former, roughly enclosed by a line running from Glasgow through Stockholm, Danzig, Trieste, Barcelona, and back to the starting point, was the Europe of steam and steel; outside the charmed circle lay "outer," mainly agricultural, Europe, steadily encroached upon by the "inner."

It should be mentioned that the second half of the nineteenth century witnessed a similar development outside of Europe. The American Civil War, the Japanese decision to emulate the ways of the West, and the Franco-Prussian War all occurred within the span of a decade. The phenomenal economic growth of the United States after the Civil War, the industrialization of Japan, and the rise of Germany are fundamental developments of the pre-1914 period, even though the impact of the first and second had not yet fully registered at the time war broke out.

If England could accommodate her growing numbers in growing comfort, it was because she managed to exchange the output of her factories for raw materials and for food. Others did likewise, if on a smaller scale. Trade is an ancient practice, but the development of industry caused its dimensions to achieve unprecedented proportions. The world of 1914 was encompassed by an immense and intricate network of economic relationships. But it is also of the highest significance that this condition had come about in a gradual, let us say natural, fashion, which led people to feel that it was permanent and stable. The barometer of economic life did indeed fluctuate, but the rhythm of the business cycle played the role of automatic regulator.

Expanding industry and trade meant growing wealth and accumulation of capital, which, in accordance with the laws of its nature, looked everywhere for profitable employment. Not only in its native home was it invested to foster further growth, but the far corners of the world felt its impact. Much British capital went into the development of American industry, for instance, just as French capital helped build Russian railways. The return on foreign investment plus that on goods exported paid for British imports. An unfavorable balance of trade was the proper condition in which Britain's economy could successfully operate, just as the reverse situation was the proper state of affairs for America, a debtor country. The assumed stability of these conditions must be emphasized, especially as the belief in their return and the failure to appreciate the meaning of their sudden disruption lies at the root of much of the financial instability that plagued the world after the war. The rate of growth of these developments was particularly marked in the second half of the century, the time when large industry, big business, large-scale finance, cartels, began to loom as dominant factors in the economic life of nations, and when London was the financial capital of the world.

This growth took place under the dispensation of free enterprise. Outside of postal service, the instances are few—railways sometimes —where the state owned and operated enterprises. The function of the state was essentially regulatory, a fact nevertheless of importance, especially where trade is concerned. The free trade view, of which Britain, though not Britain alone, had furnished the staunchest exponents, had not prevailed elsewhere. Especially in the latter part of the century protectionism was the dominant trend, until even in Britain voices were raised to question the validity of the free trade approach. The German "marriage of steel and rye," the conjunction of agricultural and manufacturing interests, was a characteristic expression of the more prevalent doctrine of protectionism. The model of the obvious benefits of a large free trade area, such as the United States, could not overcome entrenched national interests. Most enlightening is the case of the German *Zollverein*, which, having achieved precisely this condition, to the benefit of the Germanic world, turned protectionist vis-à-vis the outside.

It is sometimes said that we are now all Marxists. In the sense that the preoccupation with matters economic fills much of the current horizon, this may indeed be granted. Yet it is well to recall the ancient platitude that man does not live by bread alone. The world offers even at present many situations that may in economic terms be called absurd, for which politics or sentiment alone offer plausible explanations.

The origin of the practice of representative government may, in point of time, be credited to England. Yet it is also true that it was the great Revolution in France which, for the larger European world, signalized the destruction of absolute monarchy. Imperial Napoleonic France did much to spread abroad the ways and the ideas of the Revolution. However much things may seemingly have been restored to the old pattern at Vienna in 1815, they could never again be the same. In retrospect and brief summation, much of the nineteenth-century story of the politics of Europe lies in the struggle for the recognition of the Rights of Man, the people as the source of rightful government—in short, the democratic idea. From this standpoint it matters relatively little how "the people" are defined, for once a measure of representation is introduced, qualifying restrictions on the franchise can be removed with relative ease. The struggle was to a large extent successful. The details of its ups and downs, the temporary setbacks that were suffered, cannot and need not be considered here. The whole tale is adequately summed up in the observation that the victors of the First World War thought of democracy, for which the world was to be made safe, as the unopposable wave of the future.

Yet the goal was far from realized in 1914, and if the trend was clear, the struggle was still a central aspect of the politics of European states. France alone among major states was styled a republic, monarchy being the rule elsewhere, but the monarchical form of government bore increasingly remote relation to the question of the real locus of power. Britain, France, Italy, and some smaller states had parliamentary governments. This meant that, in contrast with the American practice, there was no governmental separation of powers; the elected legislature—at one remove the people—held instead virtually total power.[2] These, it will be noted, are the Western European states, appropriately so in view of the fact that the home of the democratic idea was English and French. In France universal manhood suffrage had been the practice since 1848; in Britain few restrictions remained, and Italy was moving in the same direction. The agitation for female suffrage had even begun in some places.

In terms of political practice, mid-Europe was a halfway house. In both Germany and Austria-Hungary the executive, the Crown, was still constitutionally supreme, but the voice of the German Reichstag carried increasing weight and the same applied in Austria. It is one of the nice posers of history whether, had it not been for the war, constitutional changes to fetter the Crown would not have shortly taken place in Germany.

The Russian Tsar may still fairly be called an autocrat before 1914, and even more the Ottoman Sultan, certainly in contrast with other rulers. Yet it is significant that in connection with the Japanese War the Tsar was moved to grant elections and a Duma. Restricted as the powers of the Duma were, emphasis must be put on the significance of its very existence. Even on the shores of the Bosphorus, Western ideas had penetrated to the extent that in 1908 the Young Turks extracted from the Sultan the establishment of an elected parliament.

One important generalization may be made. Allowing for such qualifications as the greater economic development of Germany in comparison with Italy, for example, the correlation is close between the state of economic development and that of representative institutions.

---

[2] The British House of Lords and the Italian Senate were not elected bodies, but their power was essentially a restraining one. The successful curbing of the power of the Lords had been one of the central issues of British politics in the decade before 1914.

But if this last connection may be cited as an illustration of the relationship between economics and politics, national sentiment fits into economic reality less easily. The existence of diverse peoples is an ancient fact, but the view that the nation should be the basis of the state is relatively recent. For good or ill, however, it has struck deep root, and the nineteenth century is the time during which it was raised to its currently exalted status. Strangely enough, it was the French Revolution, a movement of initially universalistic intent, that gave nationalism its greatest boost—yet, in a way, not so strangely, for it was one of the central aspects of that episode to seek to place the source of sovereignty in the people instead of in the monarch. In the process of identifying state and nation the Atlantic countries had led the way, Spain, France, and England having achieved their modern shape, essentially retained ever since, as early as the sixteenth century if not before. It was otherwise in mid-Europe, where the concept of larger unity, the Holy Roman Empire, long persisted at least in name. Napoleon finally buried the corpse and gave a great impetus to national feeling in Central Europe. Much of the nineteenth-century story of that region consists of the struggle, eventually successful, of the German and the Italian peoples to achieve unity. But the tale was not finished, for with the exception of Russia most of the Slavic peoples of Europe in 1914 still lived under alien rule.

In the mid-twentieth century the most virulent manifestations of nationalistic feeling are no longer to be found among the Western peoples, but it was otherwise a hundred, or even fifty, years ago. The normal love of native heath, patriotism, had been distorted and corrupted into aggressive assertions of superiority, the manifestations of which might seem humorous had they not led to political action. The school, at the elementary level especially, was the chief instrument through which the state indoctrinated youth.

The convergence of economic growth and national sentiment provided the motive force for the renewal of Europe's imperial activity, especially marked during the second half of the century. Outside the closed preserve of the American continent, Europe in a remarkably short time completed her conquest of the planet. Of the effects of this something more will be said presently.

Within Europe it may likewise be said that it was the conver-gence, or the simultaneous growth, of the assertion of the rights of the mass, largely a political phenomenon, and of economic expan-sion that gave the social question its new shape. The conditions of the early factory workers are sufficiently known; theirs was a dismal lot that could not but give rise to agitation for reform, to which the enlargement of the franchise gave added impetus.

Leaving aside the Utopians, characteristic of the earlier part of the century, and even the English Chartists, it fell to Karl Marx to give socialism the asset of the scientific label. The *Communist Manifesto,* issued in 1848, had little initial impact, but the Marxist idea prospered. Grounded in economic analysis and a broad view of the course of historic development, Marxism challenged the rights of private property no less than the whole structure of a society resting on those rights. In more limited terms, socialism became a potent expression and tool of the claims of the workers.

Stressing class and the conflict of classes, socialism was appropri-ately international in its outlook, even antinational to a point. Na-tional Socialism is essentially a twentieth-century contribution. The Workingmen's International was the logical expression of this state of affairs; following its collapse the second International was founded in 1889. Operating in the context of states, however, socialists organized national parties. A measure of their progress and success may be seen in the fact that by 1914 they constituted the largest single party in the German Reichstag. This was suitable expression of the degree of Germany's industrial development; in fact, allowing for the notable British exception, the correlation is reasonably close between the strength of socialism and the degree of industrial development in various countries.

Until the Russian Revolution of 1917 there is no substance to the distinction between socialism and communism, the latter word be-ing little used. But within socialism two rival groups were strug-gling for control: the reformists, who thought that the spread of the democratic practice, the franchise most of all, could result in the peaceful establishment of the new order; the revolutionaries, who contended that, whatever the verdict of the ballot, the prop-ertied classes would not surrender their privileges without resort to violence. It was also appropriate that the first of these groups was stronger in the states more advanced along the democratic path.[3]

It was mentioned above that in the latter part of the nineteenth century Europe completed her conquest of the major part of the world. The word *conquest,* however, must be taken in a very broad sense. Much of it was a simple manifestation of crude power—the partition of Africa, for example. But *conquest* also meant the subtler, though no less important, transfer of European ideas and ways over much of the rest of the world.

It matters relatively little whether this transfer was the consequence of external control and imposition of superior force or of willing acceptance, as was the case in Japan, for example. The effect in the end was very much the same, as we have occasion to see in our own time, when the very demise of empire is accompanied by continuing imitation of Western ways. Before 1914 Europe not only was mistress of most of the planet, she was in large degree its power house. For Europe was the prime home of the developments that directed the course of the world's evolution. Perhaps the sharpest illustration of this can be summed up in the word *science.* Modern science is unquestionably a European product, until quite recently almost exclusively so. With science, distinct but also related, went technology, in which domain the nineteenth century witnessed an appreciable American contribution as well. The machine in all its varied forms and applications, from steam to electricity, is a gift of the West.

This type of inventive endeavor is but one manifestation of a larger ferment of all forms of mental activity. Forms of political and social structure were the objects of active debate in Europe. Democracy, no less than the nationalistic virus, was an object of export. China is more ancient than Europe, but in her decadence she fell under Europe's influence and control. Sun Yat-sen's revolution was largely Western in its inspiration, as was the work of the Young Turks. In the domain of culture and the arts it was primarily in Europe also that the live forces of the day were to be found.

[3] In the Latin countries and among the Slavic peoples there was also an appreciable response to the anarchist tendency, of which the Russian Bakunin was one of the most notable exponents.

Europe was conscious of her place and power. And if the latter depended in the last resort on the greater effectiveness of her arms, the true bases of her influence were deeper and rested on more solid ground. The dominant note was of confidence, best voiced in the widespread belief in continued and unlimited progress. Man—European man at least—was successfully launched on the undertaking that put into his hands the key to the understanding of nature, and through this understanding he was enabled to annex and exploit the forces of nature to his own greater benefit. The confident climate was but little marred by the occasional Cassandras who were not convinced that the barometer of change was irrevocably set to "fair."

2

The Community of Europe

Before proceeding to examine the war itself, and in order to understand it, its meaning, and its consequences, we must first glance at the individual members of the community of Europe, and then sketch the relations among these same individual members, for in this last area lies the concrete and immediate occasion for the outbreak of war.

The Western Democracies

The common factor of parliamentary government in Britain, France, and Italy has already been mentioned. The executive—king or president—had been essentially deprived of power. From a parliament, chosen by popular consultation, whatever majority emerged constituted the government—a cabinet, a committee of parliament —consisting of a small group of men presided over by a prime minister, the real center of power. The government always remained dependent on the confidence of parliament, whose adverse vote could cause its fall, to be followed either by a reshuffling of the cabinet or by a general election. The parliaments were bicameral, but the lower house (Commons or Chamber of Deputies) rather than the upper (Lords or Senate) usually decided the fate of the government.

Constitutions were not always written. Such "constitutions" must rather be taken to mean the totality of arrangements that made up governmental practice, and in any event the process of constitutional change was no different from that of ordinary legislation, enacted by simple parliamentary majority, in contrast with the more elaborate American usage.

While Britain, like the United States and other English-speaking lands, usually operated under the two-party system, the rule elsewhere was a number of parties, necessitating coalitions, and hence enjoying less stability of governmental tenure.

The United Kingdom. Since 1801 the British Isles had constituted a single political unit. The very restricted franchise of the beginning of the century had gradually been enlarged until by 1914 few limitations on manhood suffrage remained and the issue of female suffrage had made its appearance. The most important of the enfranchising acts had been the great Reform Bill of 1832, the significance of which was the recognition it gave to the new force of industry. It was logical that in the next decade the equally important decision to espouse free trade should follow. During the long reign of Queen Victoria (1837-1901) Britain grew and prospered under the alternating rule of Liberals and Conservatives, between whom there was no fundamental issue on the score of constitutional arrangements.

But the challenge arising from economic development elsewhere led to some questioning of the validity of the free trade practice. The prime exponents of it, the Liberals, were split, as they were on the imperial issue. Those Liberals who came to favor closer imperial links and a vigorous policy of expansion, as well as a free trade imperial domain, eventually found their way to the Conservative fold. This happened in the eighties and nineties.

Simultaneously, the social question was becoming a more intense source of debate, and the Liberals, reversing their earlier approach, came to be the more active advocates of reform. They were returned to office in 1905, and the decade before 1914 witnessed in Britain the introduction of a substantial program of social change that even spilled over into constitutional reform, the powers of the Lords being severely curbed by the Parliament Bill of 1911. These developments gave rise to strong feeling on both sides of every issue.

Britain had long been the imperial power *par excellence,* having brought under her sway nearly one fourth of the earth. While her holdings were greatly expanded during the second half of the century, her policy was one of promoting self-government. Though relatively little was done in this direction save in the areas of predominantly British settlement, the tendency had taken firm root since the passing in 1867 of the Dominion of Canada Act.

One particular problem straddled the domestic and the imperial domains. The Irish people, having begun with moderate demands for the relaxation of British control, moved increasingly toward the demand for Home Rule. Their representatives in Parliament, in exchange for their support of the Liberal program, extracted from the Liberals promises of support for Home Rule. Dragging through several decades, the issue came to a head shortly before 1914 when the Lords blocked a Home Rule bill enacted by the Commons. Things had come to the point of possible armed resistance by the Protestant minority in the northeast of the island, and there were even some doubts about the loyalty of the army should the issue come to the test of force. Britain was sorely beset in 1914.

France. The roots of France's political problem went back to the Revolution, which had failed to produce any stability of governmental arrangements. The record of French domestic politics was troubled by a succession of revolutions and of regimes, from republic through empire, monarchy, a second republic, and an empire again. The demise of this last in connection with the defeat in the Franco-Prussian War reopened the constitutional question. The Third Republic hesitantly came into existence, but it seemed by 1914 to be securely established.

Much of French politics in the half-century before the First World War was concerned with the struggle for the consolidation of the republican regime against monarchist opposition. Once that was settled, the focus of the contest shifted to such issues as the place of the army and of the church in the state. The first largely centered on the famous Dreyfus case at the turn of the century; it was followed by the clash with the Church of Rome which culminated in the abolition in 1905 of the century-old Napoleonic Concordat, in which connection the matter of control of education also loomed large. Control of the lay state was thereafter to rest definitely in civilian hands.

Especially after the Franco-Prussian War, France also had to deal with the problem of maintaining her position in the face of the more rapid growth of others. The only European country whose population remained static, France endeavored—successfully—to find some compensation in imperial expansion. By 1914 the Third

Republic had created an empire second only to the British, though a considerable distance behind it. Empire, however, especially in economic terms, did not have for France the significance it had for Britain; the domestic resources of France are substantial, and she is unusually self-contained for a country of her dimensions.

The social question also troubled France, and a large Socialist party arose, but political control remained in moderate, not to say conservative, hands.

Italy. Italy was a very new creation. The success of the unitary solution is not to be regarded as synonymous with that of other political, economic, and social problems. The centralized uniformity of the state, following the French model, did not by itself create real unity. If there was no danger of a resurgence of the former states, the phrase "we have made Italy, all that remains is to make Italians" was apt.

The resources of the Italian land are scant, and the gap was considerable between the progressive North and the depressed South, where the low level of literacy matched the backwardness of the economy. The politics of ostensibly democratic Italy during the half-century following unification were not of the most inspiring, yet comfort could be taken from the view that, given time and peace, democracy might take firm root in Italy as well.

The Roman question had received a *de facto* solution with the final destruction of the Pope's temporal power in 1870, but Pope Pius IX and his successors staunchly refused to give legal sanction to the *fait accompli*. Nevertheless, in actual practice the Pope and the Italian King peacefully coexisted in Rome, though it took a little longer—until 1929—before the condition was formalized in a treaty.

Italy, the Benjamin of nations, naturally sought to find her place among others. She was formally acknowledged as a great power, and her policy was generally guided with skill by moderate and realistic men.

Mid-Europe

Germany. Germany, like Italy, was a recent creation and therefore faced some of the same problems, above all that of integration.

But nationalism, both German and Italian, was authentic and strong, and there was little danger that the new state would crumble.

But in contrast with the uniformity which made Italy, in terms of governmental and administrative arrangements, an extension of the Sardinian state, the federal solution was adopted in Germany, though reasons of dimensions alone sufficed to give Prussia an overwhelming place in the whole. Also, while Italian unity is properly regarded as the accomplishment of liberal Cavour, the making of Germany was unquestionably that of blood-and-iron Bismarck. Both men were, to be sure, practitioners of *Realpolitik,* but even though Bismarck had no delusions of grandeur, the fact is of the highest importance that his success marked a corresponding setback for the liberal forces which at one time had been quite strong in Germany. The primacy of the military Prussian state is an extremely important fact.

Unlike Cavour, who died in 1861, Bismarck after 1870 remained at the helm for twenty years, during which he did much to guide and mold his creation. The Franco-Prussian War had had the simultaneous effects of creating Germany and of placing her in the foremost rank of Continental states, taking the place of France in that position. The paternalistic tradition of the Prussian state was effectively perpetuated in Bismarck's direction of the country, whose growth was thereafter impressive. By the turn of the century the German challenge to the British position of economic primacy was clear, while in the field of social legislation Germany led the way, even though this may have been intended to steal the thunder of socialist agitation.

In Bismarck's view Germany was a satisfied power and her place lay wholly in Europe. He was a man of peace—after war had served his purpose—though he was not able to contain certain manifestations—imperialism, for one—of his country's expansive energy. With the accession of a new emperor, William II, in 1888, followed within two years by the dismissal of Bismarck, control fell into less able hands. Germany would now embark on a new course, her future lay on the water, and she loudly proclaimed her right to a place under the sun. In brief, the problem of Germany was precisely that of finding such a place; this put great emphasis on foreign policy, and something will be said later of the relations among European states centering on the German problem.

Austria-Hungary. The German liberals of 1848, assembled in the Frankfort Parliament, had long debated the issue of what precisely was Germany: more specifically, should or should not the German lands of the Habsburg domain be included in the prospective Germany? Bismarck had solved the question in 1866: the Habsburgs were to be excluded from Germany, their own domain left otherwise intact.

Following the Austro-Prussian War this Habsburg domain had been reorganized into the Dual Monarchy. This was the *Ausgleich* of 1867, a success of Hungarian nationalism, which gave the Magyars a position of parity with the Austrians in the new Austria-Hungary. But the Austrians and the Hungarians, in the ethnic sense, constituted minorities of the population in their respective halves of the state, the rest being made up of various Slavs—Czechs, Slovaks, Poles, and South Slavs—besides some Italians and Rumanians. These peoples, the subject nationalities, also wanted equality of status, but this was denied them by the dominant ethnic groups, especially by the Magyars. The very existence of the Habsburg state was tantamount to the denial of the nation-state, hence increasingly represented an anachronism in a time when the principle of nationality was receiving greater recognition.

The centrifugal force of disparate nationalities raised in acute form the fundamental issue of survival of the state. Especially in retrospect, it is clear that in suppression and denial could not be found a lasting answer. But there were those who hoped that timely concessions might save the Habsburg state from the fate of disruption; in particular, there was advocated a further reorganization of the monarchy that would have changed its dual composition into a tripartite arrangement, giving the Slavs a position of parity with the other two groups. But the Habsburg failing of too little and too late was destined to apply in this case also, and we shall never know what might have been. It was out of this very problem of the subject nationalities of Austria-Hungary that arose the immediate occasion of the war of 1914, of which she was to be a major victim.

Patching up expedients, relying on a mixture of ineffectual repression and inadequate concessions, depending on the time-honored practice of divide and rule, relying also on such forces of cohesion as were represented by the army, the Roman Church, and the bureaucracy, Austria-Hungary still contrived before 1914 to play a major role, even if a troubled and troubling one, in the affairs of Europe.

The Eastern Autocracies

Russia. Next door to Germany and to Austria-Hungary lay the vast Russian state. Russia's very Europeanness has been questioned, for she stretched from the Vistula to the Bering Strait. Yet, if her major part lay physically in Asia, there is little question that the basic core of the people and the physical location of the centers of power were European. The fact of size needs emphasis—Russia was and is the largest single state on earth—as well as that of the steady expansion which establishes a certain similarity between the Russian and the American cases. Both may be called imperial, yet both differed from other empires, for the fact of territorial contiguity made it possible to integrate new acquisitions into the initial core. Much of Russia's eastern expansion was directed into relatively empty Siberia, increasingly settled by Russians, but on the borders of China and in Central Asia other peoples were incorporated.

Russia had also expanded to the west, incorporating most of Poland and the Baltic lands, as well as to the south, on the Black Sea, displacing Turkish control. This steady growth in spite of the already enormous dimensions of Russia had two motives, both of them clearly pointed out by Tsar Peter the Great who launched Russia on her modern course. It is a simple and remarkable fact that, vast as she is, Russia has no good access to the sea. Peter's conquest of the Baltic lands, Catherine's push to the Black Sea, are twin aspects of the effort to reach open water. But the Black Sea and the Baltic are essentially lakes, the control of whose exits rests in non-Russian hands; hence the special importance of the problem of the Straits for Russia, particularly in the nineteenth century. Reaching the Pacific—Vladivostock was founded in 1860—and the Central

Asian push toward the Indian Ocean and the Persian Gulf are manifestations of the same urge.

But Tsar Peter's Western conquests had another motivation. He
wished to make Russia modern, which he rightly considered to
mean Western. His reforms set Russia on that path, and it was he
who brought Russia as a major factor into the affairs of Europe,
which she has remained ever since. But his reforms also aroused opposition, and Russia remained torn between the antagonistic pulls
of the progressive West and of her own peculiar nature, exemplified
by her Eastern Christianity derived from Byzantium. The varying
inclinations of nineteenth-century Tsars—Alexander I and Alexander II versus Nicholas I, for example—bear witness to this no less
than the debate between Westerners and Slavophils.

This alternating rhythm of internal direction was matched by the
alternating attempts of Russian expansion, focused at times toward
Asia, at other times toward the Balkans. Withal, nineteenth-century
Russia remained a very backward state, despite some remarkable
cultural achievements. Overwhelmingly agricultural and illiterate,
she was experiencing just the beginnings of industry and of parliamentary institutions. The highly autocratic and repressive nature
of the government put a premium on underground, conspiratorial,
revolutionary activity dedicated to violent methods of change and
to the use of terrorist tactics. We shall never know what might have
been the course of Russian development had it not been for the war,
but it may be worth mentioning the contention that a continuation
in peace of her pre-1914 economic development would have brought
her today about where she is now.

The Ottoman Empire and the Balkans. When the Turks finally
succeeded in destroying the thousand-year-old empire of Byzantium
they were a highly efficient and progressive people who, at one time,
threatened to overrun all Europe. The Habsburgs had saved Europe
from that fate just as, earlier, the Franks had stopped another Muslim thrust, the Arab. But if the Habsburg state was ill in the latter
part of the nineteenth century, the Ottoman state was more so; it
had been dubbed the Sick Man of Europe, whose demise could be
momentarily expected. The rot of internal decay that had long ago

set in had led to a virtually uninterrupted territorial retreat from the beginning of the eighteenth century. Yet the Ottoman domain was still vast, straddling Europe, Asia, and Africa, and that is what, despite its internal weakness, gave the Empire unusual importance, for its fate was a source of interest and concern to most other European states.

Attempts at reform there were, but they all failed in the face of corruption and backwardness that the Sultans, all powerful in name at least, were unable to overcome. It was in fact the inability of the great powers to agree on schemes of partition, combined with their preference for the preservation of peace among themselves, that caused them to keep the Sick Man alive. Even such an interruption as the Crimean War did not invalidate this general policy. Of this condition the Sick Man was aware, and his inglorious endeavors were directed toward the cultivation of differences among his ostensible protectors, lest their agreement result in his final extinction.

Nevertheless, he suffered losses. By 1914 all North Africa had passed under French, Italian, or British control. But a source of more serious difficulty lay nearer the center, in the remaining European part of his domain, the Balkans. The Balkans were inhabited by a variety of peoples, mainly Slavic, in addition to the Rumanians and the Greeks. These peoples had not been absorbed, with relatively few exceptions, into the conquering Ottoman society, having instead retained their Christianity, a fact of capital importance in a state where religion was the basis of law. The increasingly inefficient and capriciously oppressive Turkish rule—though the Turks were not intolerant of their Christian subjects, merely disdainful—gave rise to growing discontent. Simultaneously, the revival of national feeling penetrated into the Balkans and resulted in a struggle for emancipation. The success of that struggle sums up in brief the nineteenth-century story of the Balkans. The Serbs were the first to secure a measure of autonomy,[1] but it was the Greeks in 1830 who led others in obtaining unfettered independence. Gradually in some cases, more abruptly in others, Greece, Serbia, Bulgaria, and Rumania appeared as distinct entities on the map.

But in the first decade of the century the Ottoman state still in-

[1] There is the somewhat debatable case of Montenegro, the Montenegrins claiming that they had never been formally subject to Turkish suzerainty.

cluded an appreciable section of the Balkan Peninsula that reached
to the Adriatic and was the object of irredentist claims on the part
of existing Balkan states. A complicating element in the Balkan
situation was the fact that, as the Balkan peoples emerged into independence, rivalries among them also appeared. On a diminished
scale the Balkans reproduced the larger European picture of competing national entities. But finally, in 1912 Serbs, Bulgarians, and
Greeks managed to put aside their differences, giving for a moment
priority to their common anti-Turkish claims. Short-lived though
their agreement was, it sufficed to procure them success in the joint
war they waged against the Turks, the outcome of which was the
virtual eviction of the latter from Europe, save for Constantinople
and the Straits themselves. The failure of the Young Turk revolution of 1908 to instill new life into the decadent state has already
been mentioned.

It is important to note that Balkan and Turkish affairs were ever
the concern of the great European powers, the patrons of the small
Balkan states. If the great powers used the latter as outposts of their
influence, the converse possibility of the latter using the former for
their purposes also existed. The interaction of these opposing direc-
tions of activity is what earned the Balkans the characterization of
"powder keg of Europe." The 1914 war in the immediate sense grew
out of Balkan complications.

There were other countries in Europe in addition to the ones that
have been mentioned. At least brief reference to them should be
made, and they offer a wide spectrum of varied conditions and stages
of development.

The geographical dimensions of Spain are, by European stand-
ards, substantial, but her role had long ceased to be of importance
as her relative decline continued during the nineteenth century. Operating ostensibly under a parliamentary system, the record of her
politics and the quality of her government are uninspiring. Spain
was also troubled by dynastic difficulties, economically underdeveloped, and disturbed by revolutions and coups. The same general
conditions characterized her smaller neighbor, Portugal.

The state of economy and government was more attractive in the
northern countries. Belgium and Holland were both progressive,

well-managed states, the former more industrial, the latter more commercial, Belgium also enjoying a more liberal constitution. It may be pointed out, as a measure of her importance, that little Belgium's foreign trade was of the same order of magnitude as that of Russia.

The Scandinavian countries were all launched along the democratic path, and they were also generally prosperous, though the scantier resources of Norway made life more austere in that country than in Sweden, where a substantial industry had been developed. The two countries had been joined in personal union by the settlement of Vienna. But Norwegian nationalism asserted itself and in 1904 succeeded in procuring complete separation, a rare instance of the peaceful achievement of national independence. In the Scandinavian countries, as in Holland, the constitutional arrangements still left substantial power in the hands of the executive.

To complete the roster, Switzerland remains to be mentioned. A federation of twenty-two cantons, Switzerland was also a republic, which did not mean that her politics were radical. She offered the unusual instance of a nationality consisting of three different ethnic groups, German, French, and Italian, yet all undoubtedly Swiss. Switzerland also offered an example of orderly government and of what could be accomplished by an industrious people with limited domestic resources. Finally, the Swiss were very attached to their neutrality; located in the heart of Europe, surrounded by four major powers, they carefully avoided involvement in any but their own affairs.

3

The International Politics of Europe

Having sketched the general conditions and forces that were at work throughout the world, especially in Europe, and having indicated the nature of the circumstances that differentiated the separate units of the European community, we may conclude this introductory section by surveying the state of the relations among the European states.

The pre-1914 world was orderly and peaceful, and it was also stable, or so at least it seemed to the majority of those living in it. Though to speak of the whole nineteenth century as one of peace needs some qualification, there was no open conflict involving major European states after the Franco-Prussian War. But the effective maintenance of peace did not preclude the clash of rival and competing interests.

Moreover, it must be emphasized that the world was a world of states, and that the state claimed for itself the attribute of sovereignty. This is highly important, for in the last analysis the claim to sovereignty is tantamount to the denial of the existence of any higher authority or law. There was indeed no law, court of appeal, or other agency that could control the actions of the sovereign state. This may seem to imply a condition of anarchy in the domain of international relations. If peace rather than the law of the jungle prevailed nevertheless, it was because of two considerations. First, the freedom of action of any state vis-à-vis other states was circumscribed by the limitations of its own power. War is ever a risky enterprise; no responsible statesman would deliberately engage in war in uncertain conditions, and the governments of the European states were in general in the hands of responsible men, though of course the possibility of misjudgment or accident could never be completely excluded. Second, the authentic preference for peace had led to the acknowledgment by all that all had a right to exist. This *de facto* condition found expression in the Concert of Europe. This was no formal institution, only a tacit understanding, yet one far from devoid of reality. In simple form, since power is paramount, it was the common responsibility of the powers of Europe—the great powers that is—to preserve the international order. These powers had a right to a voice in all problems, in contrast with the smaller powers with limited and localized interests. The instances are numerous of the successful operation of the Concert of Europe, from the emergence of Belgium and Greece to independence in 1830 to the final settlement of the Balkan Wars in 1913. At Vienna in 1815 Tsar Alexander I had even thought to formalize the Concert, but his Holy Alliance, if not devoid of significance, never achieved greater status than that of limited, informal consensus. The idea was ever abroad of extending the scope of international law, but nothing was really achieved in the domain of curbing the sovereignty of the state. Many treaties were made, which constituted the nearest approach to a law of nations, but even the clear breach of treaty obligations could incur no more than moral condemnation unless others thought it fit to use force. Power was in the end the last and only resort.

Clearly, power that was too great might constitute a threat to all; Napoleon had demonstrated that. Therefore there was also general agreement on the desirability of maintaining an equilibrium of forces, a balance of power, as the best guarantee of the independence of all. But this too, if an important concept or condition, was no more than that, never a formal institution. Nevertheless, the Concert of Europe and the balance of power were far from ineffective realities, and they went a considerable distance toward insuring at least some measure of order in the functioning of the community of sovereign states. It is precisely the break in this long-established condition of the European state system that makes the First World War so important.

Within this area of agreement the pursuit of individual interest went on. Defense and the promotion of the national interest are the proper primary concerns of any government, more especially of the foreign office. Amid shifting relations there were some that over a long period of time had achieved a measure of at least seeming fixity. Britain and France had long been rivals, a relationship confirmed by Britain's role as the staunchest backbone of the anti-Napoleonic coalition. Britain had had her way, and the arrangements of Vienna confirmed her primacy in the maritime and imperial domains. Yet it is worth calling attention to the fact that Castlereagh had been strongly opposed to any diminution of France after 1815: France should remain *in* France, but she was an indispensable component of the equilibrium of Europe that others might equally upset. Napoleon's demonstration of power rated France first place among Continental states even after his defeat, but Britain was the first without qualifications.

However, the whole nineteenth century witnessed a steady decline of the French position in comparison with others, and the Franco-Prussian War was the registration of the displacement of France by the new Germany. Thereafter, though less clearly, the British position of primacy was also increasingly challenged, by Germany most of all. Thus, while the Anglo-French rivalry continued and even flared up to the edge of war in 1898, it eventually became attenuated. Within six years of Fashoda the Entente Cordiale was born, the main significance of which must be seen as a convergence of the increasingly defensive position of both countries in the face of the rising power and ambitions of others. But at the time, in 1904, this condition was somewhat obscured by the fact that both Britain and France were still aggressively expanding their empires. Not surprisingly, the legacy of Anglo-French difference survived, at least as a psychological factor, long after the reality had changed.

It had been a traditional French policy to seek reinsurance against power in Central Europe by working in alliance with whatever other power existed in the East. Sweden, Poland, the Turks had filled this role, even Prussia at one time. But the rise of Prussia, especially after 1815, and the making of Germany in 1871, the concomitant of French defeat, made that new country the focus of French fears. In even more concrete terms, the territorial annexation[1] that followed that war—it has been described as "worse than a crime, a blunder" —furnished thereafter a sharp focus of irreconcilable difference. The

[1] The case of Alsace is a very special one, especially in an age of nationalism. For Alsace was initially Germanic land but offers the rare illustration of a people changing its national allegiance. The representatives of Alsace, in the French Assembly first, then in the German Reichstag, protested the annexation.

official French doctrine, from which no government could deviate, remained that the wrong of 1871 must be undone. The issue of Alsace-Lorraine remained as a festering sore that prevented any normalization of Franco-German relations. The growth of Germany and the increasing discrepancy of power between herself and France made accommodation more difficult than ever.

Poland was gone, Sweden had become a secondary power, and the Ottoman state was sick and of little account. France accordingly turned to the new power risen in the East. But it takes two to make an alliance and the record of Prusso-Russian then German-Russian relations was too good for French diplomacy to overcome easily. It took a long time before Germany and Russia fell out, but once this happened, after the passing of Bismarck, the way was paved for a Franco-Russian understanding, which was in fact effected in the early nineties.

After the defeat of Austria in 1866, and especially after 1871, Germany was unquestionably the dominant power in mid-Europe. Bismarck had no quarrel with the new Austria-Hungary, which he instead successfully courted and turned into an ally; *Mitteleuropa* was to be an essentially Germanic preserve. But once the new Austria had accepted this view, the abandonment by her of ambitions of dominance in the Germanic world had the effect of making the southeast, the Balkans, the chief focus of her foreign policy. This fitted well into her own domestic difficulties, the problem of her disparate nationalities, among whom the South Slavs were the most restless. The very existence of an independent Serbia, a focus of attraction to the South Slavs, was a thorn in Austria's flesh.

The intensification of Austria's concern with the Balkans had another effect. For Russia too was interested in the Balkans, which lay athwart the road to the Straits. Thus the course of the nineteenth century, especially after 1867, witnessed a lasting intensification of Austro-Russian difference, the focus of which was the Balkans.

We have seen that in 1815 Castlereagh had been opposed to the diminution of France. The same considerations of equilibrium had led him to oppose too great an advance of Russia into Europe, specifically in Poland. In this he shared Metternich's view. But the focus of British opposition to the extension of Russian power came to be at the Straits rather than in mid-Europe. Thus Britain became the prime defender of the Ottoman Empire, for clearly the loss of the Straits, the site of the Ottoman capital, would result in the disintegration of the whole Ottoman state. A war was fought over that issue, the Crimean War, but what happened twenty years later, in the seventies, was not very different. An attempted Austro-Russian understanding, which turned out to be a misunderstanding, led to a Russo-Turkish war. If that conflict did not spread it was only because Russia peacefully yielded to British opposition rather than face again the test of force.

The Impact of Imperial Activity

Anglo-Russian differences were not confined to the Straits. Britain became concerned at the Russian progress in Asia—in Central Asia, at the back door of India—no less than in the Far East. It was England who, in the forties, took the initiative, by force, of opening reluctant China to the trade of the West. Anglo-Russian rivalry thus became one of the seemingly fixed points of European relations, as the Anglo-French and Franco-German rivalries also seemed to be.

But the world is not static, and these well-established antagonisms were not necessarily fated to everlasting continuance. Accommodations might be reached and lines of cleavage might change, especially as the position of power of the contestants altered. Some radical changes did in fact occur, brought about in the main by two factors: these bear the names *empire* and *Germany*. Something must be said about each.

It has been pointed out that the period after the Franco-Prussian War witnessed a marked revival and intensification of Europe's imperial activity. Britain, long established in that domain, may be said to have led the way, in the sense at least of the extent of her acquisitions. The accomplishment of the Third French Republic has also been indicated. Russia too was an old hand at the game. It was not long before Germany's bursting energies led her to join in the competition. Even relatively weak Italy felt that she must acquire what seemed to be the earmarks of great power status, though her accomplishments remained modest. And everyone is familiar with the acquisition of the Congo by Belgium.[2]

It was hardly avoidable that the imperial race should give rise to clashes of interests and claims. It was in fact the question of the Congo which caused the powers, meeting in Berlin in 1884-85, to make arrangements for the fate of that territory. The Berlin Colonial Conference in addition attempted to establish some order in the process of imperial expansion, for in this as well as in intra-European relations the powers agreed to the equal right of all to indulge in the activity as well as in their preference for the preservation of peace.

Some conflicts nevertheless could not be avoided. Perhaps the clearest of these was the Anglo-French clash in Africa, which may be seen as a continuation of the older tradition of imperial rivalry between the two countries. Clearly, it was not possible for the British to establish in Africa uninterrupted control from the Cape to Cairo while at the same time the French wished to bring under their dominance a section of Africa reaching from the Atlantic to the Red Sea.

In 1898, under the leadership of Captain Marchand and of General Kitchener respectively, a handful of French troops confronted an equally small British force. On the issue of control of the Nile Britain would not compromise. Making a correct assessment of her power and of the circumstances, France yielded. But the brink of war had been reached, and feeling between the two countries, on the French side especially, ran high. Britain did not contend that others had no right to empire, but in that domain she would have certain things whatever the cost, just as she insisted that supremacy on the sea must remain hers.

The Anglo-Russian rivalry in Asia has already been mentioned. Along a line running from Constantinople to Peking, British and Russian influences met in increasingly tighter competition. In view of the position of primacy that Britain had long held, it is only natural that the empire-building efforts of others should either meet

[2] Out of a private venture sponsored by King Leopold of the Belgians, Belgium came into possession of the large territory of the Congo, thus constituting an exception to the rule that colonial expansion in the nineteenth century was limited to the great powers.

established British positions or attempt to establish positions that Britain felt she could not allow others to hold. The necessity of defending acquired positions thus led to what may be called defensive expansion, so that imperial growth tended to feed upon itself.

Yet it was not a simple case of Britain against everyone else. For example, the mid-nineties saw a combination of French and German opposition to the British acquisition of a strip of the Belgian Congo which would have served to establish the continuity of British territorial control along the entire length of Africa. Italian imperial ambitions, centering on the horn of Africa, inserted themselves into Anglo-French rivalry. This last case, though a small one, is enlightening as one limited aspect of the larger British policy of containing or balancing the French position in Europe.

What is worth noting most of all is that as we approach 1914 imperial activity tends to become a sharper source of differences than were the rivalries within Europe herself. The best illustration of this is perhaps the case of Morocco. The French had established control over the greater part of the great western bulge of Africa, from the Mediterranean to Lake Chad and the Congo; still formally independent, Morocco was a natural object of the French imperial drive. But the Germans, latecomers in the game, also cast covetous eyes on Morocco, or at least led others to believe that such was their intention. Over Morocco two major European crises developed, in 1905 and in 1911, which threatened to result in Franco-German hostilities. Although they were in the end peacefully resolved, the long-established Franco-German enmity came to feed at least as much on the imperial issue as on the older one of Alsace.

But it is equally important to note that none of these imperial conflicts led to an open clash among the European powers. With however much difficulty, they were all resolved. Interestingly, it may be said of Europe's imperial activity that while it was the source of many differences, it also served as a safety valve for the expansive energies of Europe.

The only significant war that occurred, and that deserves at least passing mention, was the one between Japan and Russia in 1904-5. Before 1914 Japan was the only non-Western state that successfully adopted the ways of power of the West. One consequence of this development was that Japan began to evince imperial ambitions whose focus was the near Asiatic mainland of China and her periphery. Japan defeated China with ease in 1895; it is revealing of the state of European relations at the time that her success was partly undone by a combination of Russian, German, and French pressure.

But within a decade, having meantime concluded an alliance with Britain, Japan's ambitions on the Asiatic mainland collided with Russia's. The Russo-Japanese War and its outcome are significant for two reasons. On the one hand, it furnished the first modern instance of the defeat of a European state by a non-European—incidentally gaining Japan great power status; on the other, it served to reveal the seriousness of the flaws in the Russian structure. Although the Revolution of 1905 brought to Russia the beginnings of representative institutions, the following decade did not create in Russia the conditions that would enable her to withstand the impact of another major war.

Europe and the German Problem

Thus we come to a situation where intra-European problems are closely intermeshed with extra-European ones, mainly imperial, in determining the climate of the relations among the European states. The two influences may be said to have merged around a common focus, and we may appropriately conclude this introductory sketch with a brief consideration of Europe and the German problem, out of which in a fundamental sense the First World War may be said to have developed.

The nature of the German problem has already been suggested. It was the problem created by the necessity of adjustment between the stresses arising from the fact and the rate of Germany's growth on the one hand and the interests and desires of the rest of Europe on the other.

Bismarck had made Germany by blood and iron, using effectively the deep-rooted Prussian military tradition. But after 1871 there is no question that Bismarck wanted to preserve the peace. The new Germany, satisfied, could best thrive in conditions of peace. For the remaining twenty years of his tenure of office Bismarck strove to maintain order in Europe. His recipe for this was simple in formulation, if not so simple at times in execution. Germany had no quarrel with or claims against any one. She herself could maintain good relations with all, but more especially with the conservative Eastern powers. The *Dreikaiserbund,* the alliance of the three emperors—German, Austrian, and Russian—which represented in addition the defense of the social order, was the first care of his policy, successfully implemented in the early seventies.

Parliamentary Britain, because she was parliamentary, was a less dependable quantity. Britain in addition preferred to maintain a formally uncommitted position, but relations with her could continue to be as good as they had usually been in the past; Britain was not opposed to a united Germany, and the climate of Anglo-German relations remained generally satisfactory. As to France, it was up to her whether to become reconciled to the result of the last war or to nurture a grievance. Bismarck would have preferred the former, but in any event France alone was no danger. The continued isolation of France was another aspect of Bismarck's policy of maintaining good relations with others; it was a guarantee of the preservation of peace.

But although Bismarck may have dominated the international scene in his time, he could not control the relations of others among themselves. Anglo-French and Anglo-Russian antagonism were to him wholly satisfactory conditions that could help maintain the equilibrium, and he could even afford to express a measure of support for Russia's Balkan ambitions in the confidence that Britain would frustrate them at least at the Straits.

In the Eastern Question Germany had no direct interest, but the Balkans were of considerable concern to Bismarck, for they were the clear focus of Austro-Russian difference. He spent much effort on the attempt to drive that recalcitrant team in harmony, but his eminently rational solution of dividing the Balkans into two equal spheres of influence, a Russian and an Austrian, proved in the test impossible of realization. During the second half of the seventies, and again ten years later, the would-be partners fell out with each other, and for that matter the Balkan states themselves were not always amenable to great power control. Bismarck fell back on a firm alliance with Austria while striving, with a measure of success, to maintain his own connection with Russia.

In the somewhat comparable case of the Austro-Italian antagonism, the Bismarckian solution was again an alliance, the Triple Alliance of 1882, which had the further advantage of insuring that Italy would not join the French camp.

There may be said to have been two flaws in the Bismarckian system. One was the very success of his Germanic creation, whose subsequent growth he himself fostered; the other, more concrete and limited, was the exclusion of Austria from the Germanic world. The result of making the Balkans the sole focus of Austrian policy was a well-nigh inevitable exacerbation of the Austro-Russian relationship.

But perhaps the greatest obstacle to the continued success of the Bismarckian system was the absence of Bismarck himself after 1890, the period of Wilhelmine Germany. It is a fascinating, if idle, exercise to speculate on what the course of events might have been had Germany continued under the guidance of Bismarck, or of another Bismarck. No doubt certain gratuitous mistakes would have been avoided, though the continued economic expansion of Germany could hardly have been contained. Of necessity that growth constituted a challenge to others, to none more than to Britain. And it is also a fact that even before 1890 Germany had embarked on the course of empire and was developing interests of her own in the Near East.

In any case, it is incontrovertible that at a time when moderation and deftness were more essential than ever the quality of German leadership sadly deteriorated. The collapse of the delicately balanced tightrope-walking act began almost immediately after Bismarck's dismissal from the Chancellorship; the next fifteen years were a somewhat confused time of transition at the end of which Europe emerged in a totally different state of equilibrium.

Three basic assumptions underlay the course of German action: the impossibility of the composition of either Anglo-French or Anglo-Russian differences and the unlikelihood of a Franco-Russian connection. All three were to be proved wrong, and the irony lay in the fact that it was in large measure German actions which procured that result.

The dismissal of Bismarck coincided with the abandonment by Germany of the Russian connection, Bismarck's intricate Rein- *security* surance Treaty of 1887. Russia was understandably disturbed. This, together with some other Russo-German difficulties and the French readiness to seize an opportunity, resulted in the Franco-Russian alliance, the focus of which could only be Germany, or Germany plus Austria. It was a fragile reed at first, for in other respects the new allies had divergent interests and represented opposite poles of domestic political orientation.

Next and more serious was the Anglo-French connection. Britain was concerned about the increasingly successful economic growth of Germany and the resulting commercial competition, but Germany's decision to become a major naval power counted more. The first British reaction was to seek accommodation. From 1898 —this was the year of Fashoda, well designed to confirm the German view of things—to 1901 attempts were made to reach some understanding. But Germany badly misjudged. If Britain was aware of her relative diminution of place, hence desirous of cutting her world-encompassing commitments, she was not so reduced as to agree to *any* terms, nor was Germany, in Bülow's unwise phrase, *arbiter mundi*. The negotiations failed, and Britain looked elsewhere.

The Anglo-Japanese alliance dates from 1902; it was of limited scope, dealing mainly with the Far East. But France was watchful and active. The 1904 Entente Cordiale agreement was far from being an alliance, confined instead to the liquidation of imperial differences. It was not less meaningful for that. It is of great significance that it was made during the very time of the war between Japan, Britain's ally, and Russia, France's ally. Although in retrospect the course of events seems clearly set, the measure of fluidity that still existed at the time must be borne in mind. Italian behavior is a good reflection of the shifting lines of alignment. In 1902 Italy exchanged with France letters which voided her membership in the Triple Alliance of much of its meaning, but she simultaneously renewed the alliance.

There remained to establish only one more connection, the

Anglo-Russian, before all three basic assumptions of German foreign policy would be disproved. This was done in 1907, when Britain and Russia concluded an agreement dealing with Asia, similar in both spirit and content to the Entente of 1904. These agreements, to repeat, were not alliances, but mere liquidations of differences, alleviations of responsibilities, the better to concentrate power on the main focus of concern—Germany. From 1907 on Europe was divided into two rival camps, the Triple Entente, much the looser structure, facing the Triple Alliance, one of whose members, the Italian, was an increasingly doubtful asset to its partners.

Germany was understandably concerned; she felt that she was being encircled, which indeed she was. That she entertained deliberately aggressive intent would be difficult to establish. Yet her actions tended to convey that impression to others, and she was thus herself the most effective forger of her own encirclement. The picture of reality, true or false, is of greater importance than the reality itself.

The Moroccan crises are a perfect illustration of Germany's conduct of affairs. For all that she ostensibly pretended to welcome the liquidation of Anglo-French differences, Germany was desirous of knowing more about the precise nature of the understanding. She proceeded to test the Entente by raising the Moroccan question. Her basic plan was simple and quite sound. Suspecting that Morocco would soon fall under French control, an outcome that she did not regard as unreasonable, she wished, quite legitimately, to secure a price—the best possible price—for her assent. But by conveying to the French the impression that Germany might go the length of war over Morocco, Bülow's saber rattling achieved a Pyrrhic success, for he conveyed the same impression to the British and to others. At Algesiras, where the powers met to regulate Moroccan affairs, Germany found herself virtually alone, and by that time, in 1906, the Entente had turned into a much closer connection than its makers, the British especially, had intended. They and the French initiated military conversations. The second Moroccan crisis, in 1911, was largely a repetition of the first, and the final Franco-German agreement, instead of liquidating a difference, left in its train rancor, suspicion, and bitterness.

There is neither room nor necessity to rehearse in detail the intricacies of the European international scene in the last years before 1914, but one more episode deserves mention. Following a loosely and ill-contrived Austro-Russian understanding in 1908, Austria proceeded to the unilateral annexation of Bosnia and Herzegovina, occupied and administered by her since 1878 though still formally under Turkish title. The substance of the change was small, though undoubtedly Austria had breached the terms of the international Treaty of Berlin. Russia objected, but Austria in the end had her way for two reasons. One was the fact that the other two members of the Triple Entente, Britain and France, declined to give Russia strong support; the other was that Germany gave her ally, Austria, the strongest of supports, virtually threatening Russia with war.

The outcome of the Bosnian crisis was definitely a diplomatic victory for the Central Powers. But it too, like Morocco, was an empty success. Russian resentment was in the end directed more against Germany than against Austria, and if Russia was displeased at the weakness displayed by her French ally, she also felt that the alliance was more than ever essential to her, far more so than when it had been initially concluded.

To the Bosnian annexation there was a minor, yet significant, footnote. Serbia disliked the annexation of land inhabited by kindred South Slavs, a focus of her own irredentism. It required the threat of an Austrian ultimatum to secure her formal agreement. Serbian nationalism had henceforth two foci of irredentist hope, the Turkish and the Austrian. The above-mentioned Balkan Wars of 1912 had the effect of eliminating the former.

These wars may also be regarded as the last instance of the successful operation of the Concert of Europe. It was Austria again that was the chief objector to the acquisition by Serbia of land along the Adriatic. The powers met and devised a settlement different from the one contrived by the Balkan allies. One result was to destroy the Balkan alliance, but the great powers in the end had their way. The bitterness of Serbian feeling toward Austria was further intensified; it was in June 1914 that some young South Slavs murdered in Sarajevo the heir to the Austrian throne. How war broke out at this time will be examined presently in greater detail.

Yet it is well to remember that there was nothing fated about such an outcome. There had been many crises before, and they had always been resolved. There were in fact those who contended that the great civilized powers of Europe had reached a point where they had learned to find accommodation without resort to the crude, uncivilized test of force. There was even the argument that they were possessed of such powerful engines of destruction that civilization could be destroyed if by chance these weapons were unleashed. The suicide of Europe was unthinkable, and the view then prevailed that the possession of arms was the best guarantee of peace. Before 1914, as again now, was honored the old maxim, *si vis pacem para bellum;* we now call it balance of terror. The Cassandras, who proved right in the reckoning, represented exceptions to the prevalent belief in the continued course of peaceful progress.

The "accidental" interpretation of what happened in 1914 is quite as tenable as that of "inevitability," and one must guard against the distortion inherent in historic explanation. The task of history is not to assess might-have-beens but rather to explain how and why that which did happen happened. To this we may now turn. Europe was not destroyed, but Europe and the world after 1914 could never again be what they had been before. The abrupt termination of a long-existing way of life is a large part of the significance of the First World War.

II

The Performance

II

The Performance

The War

1

The Summer of 1914

Classically, the summer months have been found the best suited to military operations; armies take up winter quarters to await the return of more favorable weather. When war broke out in August 1914 it was commonly expected that the combatants would be home by Christmas. Modern techniques—because of their power of destruction, for one thing—could not possibly be used for an extended period. But modern techniques, as it turned out, were to sustain through four uninterrupted years an unprecedented amount of destruction which yet did not succeed in destroying, save in one backward instance, the fabric of society or the state. The consequences of this unplanned performance were commensurately profound.

The assassination in Sarajevo, on the 28th of June, of the heir to the Habsburg crown was a sensational event, yet no more so than many another similar deed of violence perpetrated before or since. That it was a manifestation of South Slav discontent was clear, and that the problem of nationalities was a major source of concern to the Austro-Hungarian state was well known. No less than the existence of the state itself was at stake in that issue; the observation had been made that when the Sick Man of Europe died his place in the sick bed would be taken by the Danubian monarchy. How to deal with the problem had often been discussed in Vienna and in Budapest, where there were advocates of thoroughgoing repression as the most suitable approach. That Serbia by the very fact of her independent existence, an abetting focus of South Slav unrest,

39

constituted a threat to the Habsburg state was also true. Austro-Serb relations had been tense for a number of years, especially since the 1903 coup which had shifted the position of Serbia from one of subservience to Austria to that of a Russian outpost in the Balkans. That from this state of things should be drawn the conclusion that Serbia should be taught a lesson, the Serbian danger dealt with once and for all, may be considered logical deduction. It was in any case the view that prevailed at the time, and it was made concrete in the decision that the lesson should take a military form. In this context, the attempt to place the responsibility for the Archduke's assassination at the door of the Serbian government dwindles into the relatively secondary place of occasion or convenient pretext.

In the existing state of European relations, this decision raised at once two questions: Would Russia remain passive? If not, what would Germany do? The latter country was consulted first and, rather rashly, unquestioningly endorsed any Austrian action. The significance of this step is considerable, for it meant the surrender of the control of German policy to Austria, the stronger to the weaker—the very opposite of Bismarck's view of the alliance. Then it appeared that Russia was determined to resist the Austrian resolution, but as events moved relatively slowly in 1914 it took a month for the shape of things to unfold.

By late July the crisis was indeed severe and Germany was having second thoughts, but in the extremely delicate balance of power that existed she saw no way out of her commitment without a loss of face that she would not accept. Moreover, the technical aspect of the situation was diminishing the room for diplomatic manoeuvre; mobilizations and the element of time were looming as increasingly important, perhaps decisive, considerations. The outcome was a German ultimatum to Russia, followed by a declaration of war when Russia refused to demobilize. This was on August 1.[1] Thus, out of an Austro-Serbian quarrel, fundamentally out of an Austrian domestic problem, the first open clash between major powers was that between Germany and Russia, neither of them prime movers. Yet this was in a sense quite fitting, at least sym-

---

[1] The first formal declaration of war was that of Austria-Hungary against Serbia, on July 28. There were still after this some efforts to localize the conflict, but they obviously no longer had point once major powers had become involved with each other.

bolically so, for it points neatly to the fact that, taking Europe as a whole, the central problem was Germany far more than Austria.

The larger network of European connections meanwhile came into play. Just as Russia decided on this occasion that she would not countenance a repetition of the humiliation of six years before,[2] so France, in contrast with 1908, decided that Balkan complications might warrant the risk of her own involvement. This attitude was the expression of the French view of the trend of development; certainly Poincaré, the French President—he happened to be visiting St. Petersburg in July—was definitely wedded to the view that Germany respected force alone. The issue involved in this judgment is what we nowadays debate as appeasement; clearly there is no point in seeking to appease the unappeasable, for concessions will only whet its appetite and prepare a later confrontation in less favorable circumstances. At all events, so France judged at this time and staunchly stood by her Russian ally, in a manner somewhat comparable to that in which Germany stood by Austria, though there was no element of levity in the French decision. Time being precious, if it should come to Bismarck's nightmare of the war on two fronts, Germany also took the initiative of a declaration of war against France.

Nightmare as the two-front war may have been, there were preparations for it that were in Germany considered adequate. The plan was a preview of 1940: a massive blow directed at the West, a blow whose aim was the total destruction of the French military machine; the slower-moving Russians could then be dealt with in their turn. The scheme was rational but ran into one major obstacle—the French border fortifications, the reduction of which, taking time, might rob the plan of its principal merit, prompt realization, since time was of the essence.

There was, in the German view, but one solution: avoiding the French fortifications by a northeastern flanking movement. This was the Schlieffen Plan. But here another obstacle arose, though of a different nature, for the scheme could only be accomplished by marching through Belgium, of whose neutrality Germany among others stood guarantor.

Today's world has become relatively inured to the breaking of

[2] See p. 35.

commitments of this nature. But it must be remembered that we are dealing with 1914, the terminal point of a century of at least relative international order, the very durability of which had contributed a high degree of validity to international obligations. The sanctity of treaties did not seem an empty phrase in 1914 when Germany played a powerful role in initiating the destruction of the existing order. For the view taken by Germany at this point was that necessity is the higher law, bolstered by the contention that history is written by the victors. Following upon an ultimatum that Belgium properly refused, Belgium was entered by the German army.

This decision had immediate and very serious consequences, for it produced unity among the British people, who could now join in the defense of a concrete British interest—the independence of the Low Countries—with the high moral purpose of defending as well the validity of international obligations. Britain, for all her gradually increasing involvement in the Triple Entente, was after all free of formal treaty commitments, and if the government had come to the conclusion that British intervention was necessary, the larger reaction, in country, Parliament, and even the Cabinet, had been one of considerable uncertainty. To be sure, the government's decision was based on the basic fact of British interest—preservation of the European balance of power—in turn derived from an estimate of German power and intentions. But this remained loose, vague, and debatable; the Belgian situation resolved all doubts. For there was no turning back by Germany at this point, the German Chancellor being content with the unwise expression of regret that Britain should choose to fight for "a scrap of paper." Thus Europe—all the major powers but one,[3] plus Serbia and Belgium —was at war in the beginning of August.

Much has been written on the question of the causes of the war, its origins, both long term and immediate, and a library has grown out of the discussion of responsibility for its outbreak at that particular time. Crises were, after all, familiar fare to Europe, and the one that grew out of Sarajevo was not intrinsically less capable

---

[3] Italy, on the plea that Austria-Hungary had violated the conditions of the alliance, declared her neutrality on August 3.

of resolution than many an earlier one. Allowance may therefore be made for the accidental, but it does not belong in this discussion to rehearse the details of the diplomatic activity of July 1914. The fact nevertheless is significant that so much time and effort should have been spent on the analysis of that activity, for it is a measure of an early awareness of how important an event the war really was. Taking the larger view, it may be said that, given the stresses of the whole European scene, the breach of the peace was a quite logical development. Put it another way: the little Eurasian peninsula that was Europe, which had conquered the world and was its power-house, contained too much energy and power for the narrowness of its confines. The very process of imperial activity had simultaneously furnished occasion for clashes and crises and served the function of safety valve for the overflowing energy of Europe. There was, in 1914, no more room in the world for fresh conquests.

The immediate occasion for the war was, in one of its aspects, the clash of Austrian and Russian interests in the Balkans, one manifestation of imperial rivalry. But, as mentioned before, the Balkans are in Europe, a borderline case, and the typically European force of nationalism certainly had powerful effects in them. Even more narrowly, the first cause was the Austro-Serbian difference, a most obvious illustration of the problem of nationalism.

The general reaction to the outbreak of war in fact showed convincingly how strong national feeling was everywhere in Europe. For alongside the realization that disaster had come, the experience of war had been alien to Europeans for two generations; this, and the general belief that the duration of the war would be brief, made possible the manifestation of considerable enthusiasm. The troops, bedecked with flowers, entrained to the accompaniment of bands and cheering crowds, while the cries of *"Nach Paris," "à Berlin,"* and their equivalent elsewhere, echoed across the borders of Europe. Even that inter- and antinational force that was socialism, source of concern to the governments, collapsed in face of its nationalistic rival; everywhere socialists in 1914 gave first priority to their respective national allegiances. They could in Germany contend that tsarist autocracy was the enemy, a villainous role that Prussian militarism filled equally well for the French. There was validity in both contentions.

A war may end in one of three ways: with the conclusive victory of one side or the other, or in some compromise of stalemate between the two. There is little warrant for thinking that the war was but the culmination of a deliberate and conscious German plan for the conquest of Europe; yet in a deeper sense there is truth in this view, in that, given the rate of German growth and the problem of adjustment to which that growth had given rise, there seems little question that victory would have placed Germany in a hegemonic position in Europe. Was not this possibility the fundamental reason for the British intervention? Conversely, an Allied victory could have opened the gates to a greatly enhanced Russian position. For it must be remembered that by 1914 Britain and France were essentially satisfied powers, already in defensive positions, wishing to hold their threatened own, while backward, inefficient Russia constituted an untapped reservoir of undeveloped potential. We shall see the manifestations of this state of affairs during the war itself. Colonel House's observation in 1915, which took a rather dim view of the alternative prospects of either German or Russian total success, was perceptive.

All this, however, was the future unborn. For the present, a war was being waged, an operation ever rife with uncertainties. The contending camps had for some time been in a state of rough equilibrium. For the long term, if one made a survey of resources and potential, those of the Allies far exceeded those of the Central Powers, but what counted in August 1914 was power in being rather than mobilizable potential. In this respect the Austro-German combination possessed the advantage—a compact bloc with internal lines of communication, in addition to which Germany was technically better prepared. The Allies in contrast were widely scattered. The great power of Britain would be initially of little use; Paris, as had properly been observed, could not be defended by the British navy, and the British army was of comparatively negligible proportions.

It was rational for Germany to seek to capitalize on the immediate advantage. The solution, the Schlieffen Plan, has been mentioned, the consequence of which was to make the opening of the war a Franco-German encounter. The French had wisely decided to respect the neutrality of Belgium, though their failure to make provision for countering the probable German strategy—their concentration toward Alsace—is less understandable. The German war machine rolled through Belgium, meeting some resistance and a small though important delay. Breaking through the Franco-Belgian frontier, it rolled on at a surprising pace (war in 1914 was not mechanized) toward Paris. Its object, rightly, was not to overrun territory, but to destroy the French army. But the latter, though mauled, retained its cohesion, and the imperturbable Joffre decided to make a stand at the Marne.

The clash of two exhausted forces at the beginning of September had qualities of epic that have often been told. The Battle of the Marne rates as one of the important engagements of history, comparable in significance to the 1940 Battle of Britain. Both were in a sense negative accomplishments, but the significance of both is the same—the failure of a German plan. The Germans were not so much defeated as checked and pushed back a certain distance. But it mattered less that, when an equilibrium of forces was established, they were in control of nearly all of Belgium and of a valuable sector of France than that their calculations had failed.

For Germany it must be the war on two fronts after all. The Russians mobilized rather more expeditiously than expected, and although they suffered a severe setback in East Prussia they made a useful contribution in relieving some of the pressure on the Western front. However, to repeat, Germany was not defeated; in the narrow and immediate sense she still held the military advantage. The main result of the first two months of the war, apart from the frustration of German calculations, was to prove the falsity of everyone's expectations, most of all that of the brief duration of the conflict.

Militarily, a stalemate had been reached. It took the form in the West of an extension of the line of battle until a solid front of some 400 miles was established that reached from the North Sea to the border of Switzerland. Much the same happened in the East, where a solid front ran roughly along the Russian frontier with Germany and Austria-Hungary.[4] On the fronts the belligerents dug into their positions, and trench warfare became the characteristic form of the

[4] The Austrian forces that could be spared to fight against Serbia were unable to subdue that country, which consequently continued as an active belligerent until it was overrun late in 1915.

First World War. It was a war of enormous carnage, and it revealed unsuspected reservoirs of fortitude in the flesh of man; of that aspect of things and of some of its consequences something more will have to be said. It was a war of siege on an unprecedented scale, the heart of Europe—Germany and Austria-Hungary in their totality—a vast beleaguered fortress.

It was to be also a war of indefinite duration, a turn of things for which none was prepared—witness the ridiculously small reserves of ammunitions very quickly used up—and for the waging of which all proceeded to improvise. Given the historical background, it was also, at first, what may be called a war of the classical or traditional type.

2

The Classical War, 1914-1916

By a classical war is meant a conflict of limited aims, such as the wars of the eighteenth and nineteenth centuries, in contrast to those which had directly issued from the French Revolution, for example. Some definite advantage would accrue to the victor, should there be any, even possibly a substantial advantage, but the fundamental structure of the comity of Europe would subsist. But the roots of a different development already existed at the beginning of the First World War.

Universal conscription was the common practice of the Continental states of Europe. Conscription was an expression of the democratic ideal of the individual's participation in and responsibility for the life of the state, as the French 1793 *levée en masse* had already asserted. Also it meant enormous armies, numbering in the millions, and thus, in one aspect at least, involvement of the entire population. Hence the importance of the appeal to public opinion. Wanton aggression would be hard to justify in such circumstances, and all the initial belligerents strongly insisted on the defensive nature of the war. This is true without qualification, however seemingly irreconcilable the conflicting claims might appear to an outsider, however diverse their validity. The mass of the people was then, as it is now, largely uninformed, even uninterested, in the details and intricacies of foreign policy, but it could be aroused to respond to the inevitable need of resisting aggression. Hence also the great stress on the moral aspect of the issue, on the wickedness of the enemy; this is the root of modern wartime propaganda, which in the First World War was developed to great heights of ingenuity as well as of irresponsibility. Since, militarily, the Germans were in occupation of much Allied territory, clearly a more fertile field was provided for Allied tales of German atrocities than the reverse. What truth there was in them—and there was some—

47

was vastly magnified, and not a little outright fabrication was resorted to as well. The consequences would come home to roost one day.

Of the purely military aspect of the war little will be said in these pages. During the First World War no great captains emerged, no novel strategy that would sweep all before it. Perhaps precisely because it was a contest between large and highly developed modern states, the war remained a slogging match that depended upon the more pedestrian test of detailed technical organization. The failure of the initial German plan held in it the seed of ultimate defeat for the Central Powers, for, given time, the far greater resources of the Allies could be translated into greater power in being. This, in a nutshell, is a summation of the First World War: the larger mass in the end crushed the smaller, but in the process of realizing this outcome much happened that had not been foreseen and that gave the war its unexpected shape and meaning.

The Western front was stabilized in the autumn of 1914. Essentially, it remained such to the end. The enormous expenditure of blood and treasure that both sides put into the effort to break through the enemy lines, the murderous offensives, all failed; they did no more than show how great were the resources of the modern state and its powers of organization. Verdun, the Somme, countless attacks of varying magnitude, were inconclusive blood baths, save that they raised the question with increasing sharpness, how long and how much would the peoples endure? The Eastern front was more mobile. By the end of 1915 all of Poland was in the hands of the Central Powers, but until the collapse of 1917 a continuous front was maintained in the East also.

Given a condition of stalemate, and barring the acknowledgment by both sides of the impossibility of achieving their aims and hence the acceptance of a return to the *status quo ante,* each side must seek for means to achieve superiority over the other. This can be done chiefly in two ways: by extracting more from their own resources—translating more of them, men and goods, into immediate tools of war—and by seeking to enlist the assistance of neutrals. Something will have to be said of each of these endeavors; it is convenient to deal first with the second of them.

No more than passing mention need be made of the Japanese intervention in late August of 1914 in fulfillment of the terms of the alliance with Britain. Eventually, Japan would play a very large role in world affairs, but not yet; the war meant to her little more than an opportunity to consolidate and enlarge her Far Eastern position, more concretely to fall heir to Germany in that quarter. Japan was now in alliance with Russia. Given the circumstances of the war, Japan had little difficulty in ousting Germany from the Far East, but she had no share otherwise in the hostilities.

Of more crucial importance to the European belligerents was the Ottoman situation. The Turks were uncertain, their counsels divided, but the position that Germany had for some time been cultivating with success in the Near East, plus an additional bit of prodding,[1] bore fruit; it was actually the Allies who took the initiative of a formal declaration of war against Turkey in November 1914.

Here was a highly important development that merits some attention. In the military sense the power of Turkey was not very great, but the Allies were hard pressed and the location of the Ottoman Empire had high strategic significance. The story of operations in Turkey may be summed up very briefly. The Allies—the task fell in the main to British, Dominion, and Indian forces—were able to perform at first a holding operation: Suez, for instance, was never seriously threatened. In time they gathered sufficient forces to launch successful offensives from Egypt and from the Persian Gulf; Lord Allenby entered Jerusalem in 1917 and in 1918 Damascus fell.

Of far greater moment were happenings nearer the center of the Ottoman Empire, at the Straits. One of the handicaps of the Allies was their scattered geographical position. In particular, if it should come to a long war, as by 1914 was already evident, the problem inherent in the economic backwardness of Russia was obvious. This meant in turn the problem of conveying material assistance to her. The Turkish intervention effectively closed the logical route of the Straits. Forcing them open would achieve the double purpose of re-establishing communications between the West and Russia while

---

[1] Two German cruisers which had taken refuge in Turkish waters were "sold" to the Turkish government. However they "escaped" into the Black Sea, where they joined in bombarding Odessa.

probably knocking Turkey out of the war. A coordinated attack on the Straits from the east and the west might seem a logical conception that the Russians would welcome. However, not only were the Russians themselves unable to make a contribution to the scheme but they viewed with suspicion an exclusively Western implementation of it; they and the British may have been allies, but Britain had long been the chief guardian of the Straits against Russian designs.

In the spring of 1915 the Allies succeeded in mounting an expedition to the Dardanelles. It was, logically, British in the main, with some French participation. The Straits are an easily defensible position, which the Turks, with some German guidance, succeeded in holding. Though the Allies came closer to success than they knew at the time, they decided to withdraw from the Gallipoli Peninsula and abandoned the whole undertaking.

But before they went to the Dardanelles, they had made a treaty with Russia acknowledging the eventual right to that country's outright possession of the Straits. The war against Germany was the main thing; its success required the continued participation of Russia. Concern about Russia's material and military possibilities, concern also about the steadfastness of her allegiance—the pro-German orientation had never wholly died in Russia—is what induced the British and the French, the former especially, to pay such a high price—how high may be judged from the whole nineteenth-century record. The Russians on their side had skillfully exploited the situation, furnishing a prime example of the role of power in the relations among states.

The Straits agreement of March 1915 was rather the beginning than the end of a story. For, clearly, if the West abandoned Constantinople, the fate of the whole Ottoman Empire was open to consideration. The Near Eastern problem was ripe for a radical solution. That is precisely what happened, and subsequent Allied discussions led to a series of arrangements for the partition of the whole Ottoman Empire. Needless to say, the implementation of these plans was contingent upon Allied victory, and Germany had no share in them. In the traditional context of power equilibrium this was a very radical arrangement. Actually, there were two distinct threads in the operation. Much of the Ottoman domain ex-

tended over Arab land, the large Asiatic region consisting of the
Fertile Crescent and the entire Arabian peninsula.[2] There were
among the Arabs by this time, especially in Syria, some stirrings
of the nationalistic feeling long familiar to Europe. Even more important, there were among Arab chieftains personal ambitions and
rivalries of a feudal character. It finally came down to negotiations
between the British and the Sherif of Mecca, Hussein; the outcome
was the revolt of the Arabs against their Turkish overlords.

The British interest may by this time be regarded as the paramount one in the Near East, and this latest arrangement fitted well
into the classical British imperial tradition. The Arabs wanted independence for the Arab lands in Asia, but in some manner, not
too precisely defined, the British would control the gap between
Egypt and India. However, there were other interests in the Near
East, French and Russian for instance, that could not be ignored.
Negotiations among the Allies led to an agreement whereby a
French zone of influence would extend over Syria and the abutting
part of Turkey proper to the north; this last area would in turn
be contiguous with a Russian one extending south of the Caucasus.
To complete the sketch, the Italians, after they had joined in the
conflict, were allotted a sphere in Asia Minor, west of the French,
roughly the southern half of the rest of the Anatolian peninsula.
Finally, mention should be made of that Pandora's box, the Balfour
declaration of 1917, which advocated the establishment in Palestine
of a "national home" for the Jewish people.

It is clear that this whole series of agreements represented a continuation of the imperial activity of the powers of Europe, as well
as a certain extension of the principle of nationality—witness the
Arab and the Jewish provisions. Also, among the chief participants,
an acknowledgment of the desirability of the balance of power,
among themselves at least; the exclusion of the Central Powers, if
understandable, was no less significant for that. The rearrangement
was far-reaching and drastic, yet no innovating deviation from the
traditional principles that had guided the diplomacy of Europe. It
will also be noted that there was a measure of overlapping in the
various claims. If the letter of them was not strictly speaking incon-

[2] These arrangements did not apply to Egypt, over which Britain had proclaimed
a protectorate in December 1914.

sistent (there were no formal treaties with the Arabs and the Jews, both of whom understood fairly clearly their position and were content to rest their hopes in the future), the same cannot be said of their spirit. Balfour's later observation was quite right—that the necessities of war lead one to do things that one would otherwise rather not do. Britain, more than any other power, stood at the center of all these arrangements.

While these developments were unfolding from the consequences of the Turkish involvement in the conflict, the war had spread elsewhere. Once Italy had declared herself neutral, resting her case on the contention that her allies had violated the defensive character of the alliance, it would have been highly awkward for her to join them at a later date. Her decision represented a judgment of where her interest lay, as well as one on the probable outcome of the conflict. It had been a fundamental tenet—and a sound one—of Italian foreign policy never to engage in conflict against England. For Italy the choice was thus between continued neutrality and participation in the war on the side of the Allies. Both possibilities had adherents who carried on a lively debate in the country, while the government endeavored to exploit the situation to the best national advantage, bargaining with both sides: How much for neutrality? What price for intervention? At the broader, popular level the ideological element intruded, conservatives being sympathetic to the Central Powers, hence favoring neutrality, as did most socialists, who adhered to the Marxist view of the war as a clash between rival capitalistic, imperialistic states. Liberal elements were generally more sympathetic to the Allies, as were also some nationalists, who saw an opportunity to complete the work of the Risorgimento and to aggrandize the country and who generally regarded war as a desirable stimulant.

The outcome was the Treaty of London in April 1915, the contract by which Italy joined the Allies in exchange for the clear and definite promise of certain advantages, mainly territorial gains and mastery of the Adriatic. Italy went to war in May, but the calculation that her weight would suffice to break the military stalemate proved incorrect; a new front came into existence from Switzerland to the Adriatic. One observation should be made here about a point which was to have later significance: Italy, as for that matter all but

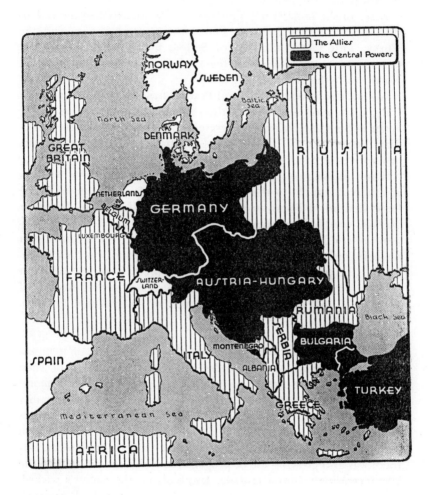

the initial belligerents, could hardly plead the inescapability of defense, but at best the promotion of the national interest, plus, to a certain point, an ideological preference.

Later in the same year a similar situation occurred in the case of Bulgaria, save that Bulgaria joined the Central Powers and the Turks. This meant the end of Serbia, finally overrun, and the uninterrupted extension of a block of territory running from the North Sea to the Persian Gulf.

No one else joined the Central Powers. But in 1916 Rumania, like Italy, abandoned her pre-1914 allies and went into the Allies' camp, again in the expectation of concrete rewards. This too, in the immediate sense, proved to be a miscalculation, for Rumania was promptly overrun.[3]

Thus, as the year 1916 drew to a close, the map of the war was generally favorable to the Central Powers, who could point to the large sections of enemy territory that they had overrun. Yet their enemies would not acknowledge defeat. If the French and the Russians especially had sustained heavy losses of life, the result in part of their initial strategies, the manpower of Britain was only beginning to be truly mobilized, while the supremacy of the Allies at sea enabled them to deprive the enemy of access to the resources of the rest of the world, which continued to be available to themselves.

The war therefore continued. But the continuation of it meant increasing demands on the peoples, to a degree undreamed of when the conflict had started. This put a high premium on the moral aspect of the struggle, for people in the mass will far more readily respond to the appeal of slogans and ideals than to the nebulous prospect of gain for a price seemingly without limit. The stress on the defensive aspect of the war remained a powerful argument. But there was also growing use of propaganda which tended to turn the war increasingly into a crusade. Emphasis on the enemy's wickedness was an obvious, though negative, device to which all resorted. But in the effort to identify the war with a contest between good and evil the various belligerents were differently placed. The Allies,

[3] With the intervention of Greece, under strong Allied prodding, in June 1917, all the Balkan countries were involved in the war.

the Western powers especially, were from this standpoint in a more favored position. Britain and France were after all the initial homes of democracy, and there was validity in their contention that they were resisting the designs of Prussian militarism; for the French, the wish to right the wrong of 1870 was a powerful stimulant. The case of Italy was weaker, though to a point the same ideological factor could be stressed and much could be made of the *irredenta*. The position of Russia was the weakest of all, made worse by the backwardness of the mass of the Russian people, who had little grasp of what positive issues they might be fighting for. How far could just loyalty to the Tsar be stretched in a country where less than a decade ago discontent with his rule had been the cause of revolution?

Nevertheless, with the Russian exception, the Allies could with a measure of validity insist that they were fighting for freedom, be it by laying stress on the more democratic form of their governments, or by emphasizing that other form of democracy, self-determination. If one agrees with the view that democracy and nationalism were two of the main currents of the nineteenth century, then, to a point at least, the Western allies may be said to have had, if not God, at least History on their side. Needless to say, they sought to make the most of this.

The corresponding disadvantage of the enemy is clear. Leaving aside Germany's mode of government and the violation of Belgium, it was a fact that Germany contained some alien peoples, Poles on one side, Alsatian French on the other, plus a few Danes, while the same was not true of any of the Western allies.[4] As to the Dual Monarchy, it was not a nation but a congeries of increasingly discontented peoples whose allegiance in the war was not even certain; there were qualms about sending Slavic units to fight against the Russians, the rate of desertion to whom, especially among the Czechs (a Czech legion was organized in Russia from their numbers) was substantial. Disgruntled nationalism was the very thing that had

---

[4] A reservation may be made in the case of Britain, owing to the unresolved Irish situation. The passage of a Home Rule bill for Ireland elicited such strong opposition on the part of the Protestant minority in Ulster as to raise the specter of possible civil war. But upon the outbreak of war, even the Irish leaders in the British Parliament initially agreed to a postponement of the effects of the Home Rule bill.

furnished the immediate occasion for the war, and Austria-Hungary was fighting for no less than her continued existence. But who, or what, was Austria-Hungary?

Yet all this may seem to bear little relation to the inter-Allied arrangements, imperial in large part, outlined above. To ask, for instance, the French people to resist German aggression, or even to die for the recovery of Alsace, was one thing; to ask them to lay down their lives for the control of Syria might elicit a very different response. The various inter-Allied agreements were not public property but, in the classical tradition of diplomacy, highly guarded governmental secrets. The ambiguity of this state of affairs hardly needs emphasizing; out of its revelation the later slogan "open covenants, openly arrived at" derived much of its popularity. It must be stressed again that the Europe of states was continuing to function in traditional fashion, its leading units looking to a possibly far-reaching readjustment of their power relations but not to the destruction of the existing system. It was a long time before the Allies came to espouse the principle of nationality in regard to the Habsburg state to the point of envisaging that state's total destruction.

In any case, it is easily understandable that increasing attention should have been given by all parties to some attempt to define their war aims. One major power alone remained outside the conflict. The reaction of the United States to the outbreak of war in Europe had been one of shock, but, as the war settled down to an indefinitely prolonged contest, the prevailing feeling of the American people may best be summed up in the phrase, "the quarrels of Europe are not our quarrels," in the limited sense a correct estimate. The American President generally took the same view. Wilson's own background was essentially domestic American in the sense that his horizon did not substantially extend beyond the American shores. The issues that had brought him to power were certainly overwhelmingly domestic, and the New Freedom had been before 1914 the main concern of American politics. Wilson, however, was highly conscious of the American position and power, facts which designated the United States as a logical mediator between the European belligerents, nor was Wilson averse to playing such a role. His alter ego and confidant, Colonel House, went to

Europe in 1915 and again in 1916 to survey the war at first hand. His earlier judgment has been cited, and there seemed in 1916 little common ground on which the enemies could meet.

In November 1916 Wilson was re-elected by a narrow margin. One of the slogans of his supporters during the campaign had been, "he kept us out of war," but that did not mean that he had abandoned the hope of playing a mediating, possibly an arbitral, role in the conflict. The turn from the year 1916 to 1917 witnessed the conjunction of what may be called two peace offensives.

Wilson was determined to pursue his mediating attempts despite the fruitlessness of previous discussions, mainly with the British and the Germans. On December 20 an American note went out to the belligerents: on the basis of their professed, but vague, declarations of purpose, it was hoped that their aims might not prove irreconcilable, if only defined with clarity, which they were asked to do. All the recipients reacted with suspicion, yet the American demand could hardly be ignored.

Its first effect was in fact a German attempt to anticipate it, for it was known that Wilson's note was forthcoming. The reasons for the German move were in part military,[5] but Germany's latest success, the capture of Bucharest, furnished an appropriate occasion. On December 12 the so-called German peace offer was launched. It was essentially a propaganda move, ostensibly proposing negotiations but carefully avoiding any concrete proposals. In their parliaments first, then officially, it was indignantly rejected by the Allies, who dubbed it a ruse and a trap and insisted that no peace could be discussed until prior guarantees had been given, acknowledgment of the principle of nationality for one. Clearly there was no possibility of the two sides coming together. As to the American proposal itself, it met with a German rejection. The Allies, though embarrassed, met in Rome in January to compose a reply. What they produced was somewhat vague and left considerable room for interpretation, but certain things were reasonably clear: in addition to the demand for full restoration of, and compensation for, the overrun territories, they clung to the demand of self-determination for the subject peoples of the Central Powers

---

[5] Germany was about to embark on unrestricted submarine warfare, the formal decision and announcement of it being made in January 1917.

and Turkey; under the conditions of 1917 it was obviously incon-
ceivable that Germany should relinquish such lands as Poland or
Alsace.

The German peace proposal and the American attempt at media-
tion had, therefore, no concrete effect at the time. They were nevertheless important, for they served to clarify the nature of the war
aims of the belligerents, a matter of significance to their own peoples, to the enemy, and to the neutral world, not least the United
States. The advantage of the Allies in this respect must be stressed,
for if they had secret plans and arrangements, the disclosure of
which would have been highly awkward, they did also stand for
certain principles of universal applicability. There were no such
principles in the enemy camp, whose aims had therefore to remain
concealed. Germany hoped to make some further territorial acquisitions at the expense of Belgium and of France, and in the former
country she did her best to promote her aims by fostering the
bilingual division between Flemish and French, along the lines of
which she instituted administrative divisions. Likewise in the East,
once Poland had been overrun, an attempt was made to enlist Polish
support through the promise of a reunited, independent Poland.
The game was too transparent and these efforts met with little response; Pilsudski, who earlier had gone as far as to raise a Polish
legion and seek collaboration with Austria, fell out with his
would-be masters and was imprisoned by them. As to the Sultan's
attempt to raise a holy war under the banner of religion, it found
some response in North Africa, in recently conquered Libya especially, but neither Britain nor France experienced any difficulty
with their Moslem subjects. There arose instead the previously
mentioned Arab revolt.

Thus, as the year 1917 opened, the prospects of peace were still
indefinitely remote and dim; both sides insisted that they would
not compromise, both were still set on victory, the shape of which
for either side was reasonably clear. Wilson had, for the moment at
least, to acknowledge failure, though he clung to his view of what
the nature of the peace should be. His assertion that it must be
reached without victory, which he made in a message to Congress
on January 22, received the same unfavorable reception on both

sides of the trenches; his Olympian detachment seemed closer to insult. There appeared to be every reason for America to persist in her policy of noninvolvement. Yet in less than three months she was involved in the conflict. To this, and to some other changes in the crucial year of 1917, we must now turn our attention.

3

The Deeper Forces Break Through

Let us recall again that in August of 1914 there was general agreement on the impossibility of a long war. This view was based on a mistaken appraisal, a pessimistic underestimation, one may say, both of the human capability to absorb punishment and of the depth of the reservoir of economic resources.

In keeping with these expectations, Britain thought to carry on business more or less as usual, no doubt with some adjustment and disturbance, but with only a minimum of these. It took very little time for the facts to belie these calculations, but rather longer for Britain to acknowledge the necessity of drastic readjustment. Very soon the physical demands of the war forced a modification of industrial production. Britain cannot exist without international trade: she has to import vast quantities of food merely to exist, and her industries depend in large part on imported raw materials. Her mastery of the seas at first insured reasonable freedom of communication with the outside world, for the menace of the submarine did not become too serious for some time. But she soon found that she could not continue to produce and export enough to pay for her purchases. Gradually, as the war dragged on and the pressure increased, choices had to be made and priorities established between the various needs—food and materials of war, for instance. A regime of unrestricted free enterprise is not suited to meet these necessities in orderly fashion. There was nothing for it but to accept the necessity of ever-expanding controls, be it food rationing or the allocation of shipping. With the increasing seriousness of the submarine menace the controls became all the more stringent. But all this was seen in the light of an emergency, the passing of which would permit a shrinking of the power of the central government and a return to the normality of freer operation. Also, it should be pointed out that there were in 1914 no prior plans for such arrangements, which were made in response to the inescapable pressure of circumstances as the need became clear, on an *ad hoc* basis of improvisation, albeit in disciplined fashion.

Where food was concerned, France was more favored than Britain in being capable of sustaining herself; the food situation in France never became very serious. But in France the major part of the nation's industrial production was either near the front line or already in enemy hands. There was in France rather more improvisation and less discipline than in Britain, yet French industry achieved remarkable results. In France too arose the necessity of extending regulatory controls, also presumably on a temporary basis.

The war thus had the effect of greatly increasing the powers of central government, the state, a phenomenon that none could escape. In the immediate military sense, the German preparations were the best and most thorough of all. But Germany too had believed in the short war and had made little economic preparation. This was very serious for her, as she was deprived by the blockade of normal access to the outside world. For a time the neutrals provided loopholes in the blockade, and Germany also increasingly exploited the resources of occupied territories. But the food situation became very serious, the "turnip winter" of 1916 a lasting memory of misery. She too proceeded to coordinate the various aspects of her economy, in doing which her economic dictator, the able Walter Rathenau, achieved remarkable results. Her scientific resources, those of her well-developed chemical industry, for instance, were also harnessed to extraordinarily good effect; the universal vogue of the word *ersatz* dates from this performance. The whole tradition of the German state was less inimical to regulation and control than was the case in Britain and in France, and the German qualities of discipline, efficiency, and thoroughness served Germany well in this respect.

The other chief belligerents managed less well in the face of the same pressures. The poor military performance of Austria-Hungary was but another aspect of the shaky structure of the whole state; controls and regulations to be sure there were, but *schlamperei* (carelessness) perhaps best describes the quality of the Austrian performance, which must be rated poor. Italy too, when she entered the war, thought that it would end soon. A weak economy combined with a weak political structure resulted in much suffering in that country. She needed to import both wheat and coal, a fact well calculated to drive home to the Allies the need of inter-Allied organization; allocation of raw materials and shipping, for example, was extended beyond national boundaries. Such conditions produced considerable stresses, both at home and among the Allies.

Italy was fortunate in that she always remained accessible to outside assistance, else she too might have gone the way of Russia, the worst case of all by far. Russia may have been a barely qualified autocracy in which the power of the state was little hampered by political institutions, but Russia was in every sense a backward state where disorganization prevailed. Russia had been before 1914 one of the granaries of Europe, yet food came to be scarce in Russia, while, with better justification, the deficiency of industrial production was appalling. Thus we may see a rough measure of correlation between the staying power, the capacity for organization, on the one hand, and the degree of economic development of the various belligerents on the other.

Such conditions as have just been described are neither unique nor unprecedented. What was unique about them was their occurrence after a century of relative peace, and even more their intensity and duration. The First World War made truly unprecedented demands on the economies of the belligerents.

War is expensive, too, and one argument for the impossibility of long duration had been that all, before long, would be bankrupt. But this is one thing we have learned, partly from the First World War: that financial problems are but a relatively minor limitation to the pursuit of hostilities. This does not mean a lack of problems, however. Of financing the war out of current revenue there could be no question; though taxation was better handled in some countries than in others, all had to resort to vast borrowing. Printing money, inflations, mortgaging the future, provided the sinews of war. Also, to put it crudely, there was much accumulated fat in wealthy 1914 Europe, on which for a time Europe lived, emerging far leaner from the experience.

The demands of the war took other forms as well, even more dramatic and harsh, and more immediately perceivable. We are referring to manpower, the factor most directly connected with morale.

The British army in 1914 was pitiably small. It was a professional army, fought well, and was largely destroyed. Britain then made a new and larger contribution, depending on volunteer enlistment; the response was good, if eventually insufficient. The response came, as might be expected, in disproportionate degree from that section of society that provides the leadership of the nation. In addition, throughout the war the rate of casualties among officers was disproportionately high, a case of *noblesse oblige,* if one will. Much was to be said later on about the significance for Britain after the war of this depletion of the reservoir of her future leadership.

The French had a similar experience in this respect, but there was conscription in France. An important fact was the demographic condition of France, the one country with a static population, hence in relative terms a country of elderly people. France was fully aware of the growing discrepancy in numbers between herself and Germany—a two-to-three ratio in 1914—and the 1913 extension of the term of military service to three years had been designed to redress, at least temporarily, the balance. As a consequence, there was no French inferiority in combatant numbers when the war broke out. But, in addition, the French military doctrine of 1914 was wedded to the offensive, the *élan* of which would carry all before it. The application of this doctrine in the face of German machine guns came close to disaster. Lives were thrown away recklessly at first; French casualties were highest during the earlier part of the war, until the generals had learned the lesson, which took some time. The consequence was a highly sobering effect on French morale, both at the front and in the rear, where by 1915 it was the norm for a French family to have had a husband or a son killed in battle.

The Russians were in some ways even more reckless. There was in Russia, by contrast with France, no problem of numbers but rather, in view of the deficiency in matériel, a belief on the part of Russian military leaders that the weight of the Russian mass could adequately compensate for that shortcoming. The Russian mass was recklessly used and correspondingly slaughtered; quite a little of it was also captured. The impact of these tactics hardly served to exhilarate the morale of the Russian people, who were also relatively less conscious than others of the purpose of the war.

The Germans husbanded their forces better, in the earlier stages at least, but once the stalemate of the war of position had developed, the losses became more equalized. No one on either side was successful in restoring mobility to the war (the tank, as a significant weapon, came very late), and especially in the West the standard tactic was that of "going over the top" after an intense artillery preparation which invariably failed to destroy the defense.

The war by 1916 had become a test of endurance, a match of material resources of the belligerents, of their ability to transform these into immediate tools of war, shells and guns, and of the spirit of men on both sides. That year marked a return by the Germans to a variant of their initial plan, elimination of the Western front; they made an attempt, on an unprecedented scale, to capture the old French fortress of Verdun. Like the Marne, Verdun was a Franco-German encounter, and as on the former occasion the French made good their slogan, *"ils ne passeront pas"* (they shall not pass). To that extent Verdun may be described as a French success and a German setback, negative though it was in both cases. The losses were roughly equal, about a quarter of a million killed on each side, and the Germans had to begin to give some thought to the problem of reserves, especially as a similar bloodletting was taking place on the Somme, an attempt in part to relieve the pressure on Verdun. Verdun lasted six months and covered a few square miles of territory; the Somme from July to September added half a million German casualties, some 400,000 British, and nearly half that number of French.

How long could such attrition be sustained? Governments everywhere endeavored to deal with the emergency. While they did their utmost to provide in increasing quantity the military necessities of the war and to sustain the morale of their peoples, there was proper cause for their concern. The fatigue and the doubts induced among the populations found echoes at the higher levels of direction; the original enthusiasm that had brought well-nigh unanimous cooperation at the beginning of the conflict—*union sacrée, Burg-*

frieden (putting domestic quarrels on ice), and coalition governments—was showing signs of erosion.

In Germany Chancellor Bethmann-Hollweg was beset by criticism of his supposedly deficient vigor in prosecuting the war. Late in 1916 the debate centered around the issue of submarine warfare, the unrestricted use of which was advocated by Ludendorff. It was to a point a contest between the military and the civilian government; in the light of Germany's constitutional distribution of power, it is not surprising that the military had their way, with consequences presently to be seen.[1] What discontent there was and what criticism of Germany's annexationist aims—there was some —were at this time still feeble, no more than a harbinger of things to come in future.

The weaker structure of Austria-Hungary was beset by more serious trouble, the dubious allegiance of the subject nationalities and Hungarian divergences. The passing of the old Emperor in November 1916 was an appropriate symbol of the passing of an age. His young, well-intentioned, and inexperienced successor, Charles I, under the pressure of a variety of influences (that of his wife, for one), even thought that an end might be put to the conflict. The contacts he established with the French government through his French and Belgian relatives, the princes of Bourbon-Parma, were foredoomed to failure. By the Allies they were correctly interpreted as a sign of weakening in the enemy camp, but rather than being translated into a possibility of compromise, this was considered an asset to be exploited. For that matter, the British and the French were no more in a position to curtail Italian demands than were the Austrians to dispose of German-held Alsace-Lorraine. The negotiations failed and even led to publicity and recriminations; one of their ultimate effects was to confirm the German dominance over Austria-Hungary, for Charles had to go to Canossa and reassert his loyalty to the alliance. This episode unfolded during 1916 and 1917.

A situation somewhat comparable to the German developed in Great Britain. The issue there was hardly a contest between the respective places of the military and civilian branches of the gov-

[1] See below, pp. 87-88.

ernment in conducting the war, but there was dissatisfaction and weariness over the lack of vigor of Prime Minister Asquith, to which the events of 1916, especially the futile bloodletting of the Somme, gave added point. Lord Lansdowne voiced his pessimistic forebodings in a memorandum that was placed before the Cabinet. The outcome was an internal crisis out of which a more determined leadership emerged, with the displacement of Asquith by the more vigorous Lloyd George. The direction of the war in Britain was thereafter in reliable hands, conducted with efficient ruthlessness by the inner War Cabinet, a five-member group guided by the Prime Minister.

In France initial deference was given to the needs and wishes of the military. The success of the Marne naturally enhanced the prestige of the supreme commander, Joffre, who tended to be impatient with civilian direction. But, as in Britain, the supremacy of the civilian government was never in question, though the greater bloodletting of France found reflection in correspondingly greater discontent, which in turn overflowed into parliamentary expression; the original *Union sacrée* was subject to great strain. As Lloyd George emerged to the leadership in Britain in December 1916, the Briand government survived in France with no more than a ministerial reshuffling. It was to take another year before Clemenceau, a leader comparable in stature to Lloyd George, came to the forefront in France, for whom the year 1917 was to prove a very difficult passage.

Matters were even worse or looser in Italy, where the aged and ineffectual Boselli presided over the government for more than a year, from June 1916. The circumstances of the country, economic and political, have been alluded to, and the manner in which Italy had entered the war had left her a divided country. Italy had not even declared war on Germany at first—she finally did so in 1916— and the lack of enthusiasm for the war in Catholic quarters, combined with the sullenness of the socialists, was reflected in defeatism that some considered verged on the treasonable but that the government did little to combat effectively.

Toward the end of 1916 there was everywhere much weariness, but despite sufferings and doubts, even some defeatist criticism, the will of the combatants stood firm. So it appeared, at least at the level of governments and in the parliaments, where the dominant tendency was rather to demand greater vigor in the prosecution of the struggle. The case of Britain has been mentioned, and a similar feeling prevailed in the German Reichstag, which in December passed a law amounting to a civilian draft of men between the ages of sixteen and sixty, if they were not already in the armed forces. Thus, the response at that time and at the beginning of 1917 to the German peace offensive and to the American attempt to find common ground among the contestants, which has been indicated before, best sum up the mood of the belligerent governments. The same applies to the above-mentioned failure of the Austrian attempt at negotiation and to the papal endeavor in 1917.[2]

But if the war was to go on, the feelings of the masses, be they quiet or sullen resignation or the beginnings of more positive disaffection, could not be ignored. The fact should also be mentioned of a growing discrepancy between these feelings of the masses and the positions taken by their representatives; all the existing parliaments had issued from prewar elections. There were those who had very positive solutions indeed; and in this, at the time and even more in the future, may be seen one of the most significant effects of the war.

The Marxist Answer

We must go back a little in time to trace at this point a different development.

Of the growing success in pre-1914 Europe of the socialist doctrine stemming from Marx, something has already been said. The international, antinationalistic content of socialism has also been mentioned as a source of concern to the governments, as well as the collapse of the Second International after, in August 1914, the so-

[2] Following unsuccessful approaches in 1916, Pope Benedict XV issued a pontifical note on August 1, 1917 that proposed the possible bases of a just and durable peace based on reasonableness and compromise. Despite some German reservations, the papal note found a better reception with the Central Powers than among the Allies. The latter, not without justification, considered the papal proposals too advantageous to their enemies. An evasive German answer and the absence of official reply from the Allies made the papal move unavailing, like other attempts at compromise during this period.

cialists whose countries were at war had given priority to their respective national allegiances. It was otherwise in the neutral countries, where socialists could continue to adhere to the orthodox Marxist view of the war as a conflict between rival imperialistic capitalisms.

As early as September 1914 some Swiss and Italian socialists, together with some Russian émigrés, meeting in Lugano, had reasserted this interpretation, emphasizing the class against the national aspect of the contest. Meanwhile Lenin, in his organ *The Social Democrat,* stressed the socialists' duty to transform the national struggle into the class struggle. If the International had proved untrue to its faith, a new organization should be created. These were small things amid the initial clatter of guns, and in 1914 Lenin was a Russian exile but little known outside his rather narrow circle.

Following a call from the Italian Socialist party, a small group of socialists, French and Germans among them, met at Zimmerwald in Switzerland in September 1915. The appeal issued by this unofficial gathering for a peace without annexations or indemnities elicited virtually no response. Another meeting at Kienthal the following April brought together a somewhat larger socialist representation. In the lively debate that ensued, the more radical tendency of outright opposition to the war carried the day, but in the Western countries and in the Central Powers the emphasis on peace rather than on revolution still dominated the socialist movements, though signs of cleavage were beginning to appear.

In any case, socialism had begun to recover from the blow of the outbreak of war, which, if it had destroyed the International, had left untouched the various national party organizations. The more moderate agitation, that for peace, inserted itself easily into the weariness and questionings to which the endless war and its demands for sacrifice gave rise. In France, in December 1916, continued Socialist party participation in the government had been endorsed by only a small majority of the party congress, and an even smaller one had opposed the resumption of contact with other, including enemy, Socialist parties. In Germany the Spartacist group, under the leadership of Karl Liebknecht, was still very small; the main opposition to the Chancellor's conduct of the war came rather from the conservative elements, which criticized his lack of vigor in prosecuting the struggle. There was a further split in Germany, where the Independent Socialists, early in 1917, joined the Spartacists in proclaiming their desire for peace. This was not very different from the sentiments voiced in Britain by Ramsay MacDonald, also in December 1916.

There were, in addition, beginnings of labor unrest, abetted by the rising cost of living that was unmatched by rising wages. The introduction of conscription in Britain and the consequent attempt at the "dilution" [3] of factory labor produced a strong reaction from the unions, who saw in this practice a possible threat to their position. "Dilution" became so diluted as to be practically abandoned. In France, in Germany, in Italy, there were strikes, sometimes of alarming dimensions. The strikes became more acute in 1917. The increasing recalcitrance of labor and the resurgence of socialist questioning are not synonymous developments, though socialism recruited its strength mainly from labor and the trade unions were closely connected with the parliamentary parties. In any case, both tendencies received an enormous encouragement from the events that took place in a country where industrial labor was not the great mass and where socialism had but slender roots. Of the Russian Revolution of 1917—what many would regard as the most significant product of the war—some things must be said at this point.

This is not the place to repeat the details of a sufficiently well-known story, the Russian events of 1917, nor to rehearse the somewhat tiresome, and at times esoteric, debates that had been going on among Russian Marxists for some years. It will suffice to stress and to recall that the Revolution was essentially an internal collapse. The primitiveness of Russia's economic development was a deficiency that time might have made good, but hardly one that could immediately be remedied once the war had begun. The isolation of Russia from sources of supply that her allies might have furnished thus left her at the mercy of her own industrial back-

---

[3] In an attempt to increase the manpower available for military purposes, it was proposed to "dilute" skilled factory labor by making use of less qualified workers and of women.

wardness. In addition, the management of what resources there were was uncommonly poor; inefficiency, profiteering, and corruption occurred in Russia on a larger scale than elsewhere, and the political situation, at once cause and reflection of these conditions, can only be described as appalling. The Tsar was a weak man, a twentieth-century Louis XVI, little aware of the state of affairs, isolated in the distorting circle of the court, where defeatist forces could freely exercise their deleterious influence. His wife, to whom he was devoted, was among these. Mentally unbalanced, removed from reality, the Tsarina was more than anyone responsible for the degree of power that Rasputin achieved. One cannot cite a better illustration of the conditions that prevailed in Russia than the role of this uncouth but shrewd "holy" man; were it not a matter of historic record, one would be tempted to describe the episode as the invention of a diseased imagination.

The reckless use of Russian manpower did not go far in compensating for superior German equipment and direction. Had it not been for her traditional assets of size and distance, Russia might have suffered at an early date the fate that Germany hoped to inflict on the West. To make things worse, the backwardness of the illiterate peasant mass made the Russian people far more recalcitrant to the nationalistic exhortations that the governments of the West used to appreciable effect. In the face of appalling losses, to "fight for the Tsar" would soon lose much of its appeal when there had been so much about his rule that was objectionable.

By the end of 1915 the Russians had sustained substantial territorial losses. The following summer General Brusilov attempted a major offensive, the thrust of whose initial success could not, however, be sustained. Another million men were lost, and desertions attained alarming proportions. The hardships of the succeeding winter put Russia, at the beginning of 1917, in a far worse position than any of the other belligerents. The collapse was at once economic, military, and psychological, and Russia was ripe for dropping out of the war.

Yet for a time the year 1917 seemed to offer hopes of retrieving the situation. Strikes, rioting, and a mutiny of the garrison in Petrograd were the catalysts of long-accumulated discontent that precipitated revolution in March. A provisional government was organized and the rule of the Romanov dynasty came to an end, leaving the shape of the future to be settled by a constitutional assembly.

The March Revolution, not altogether a surprise, was not unwelcome to Russia's allies. The fact that the constitutional parties of the Duma dominated the provisional government led to the expectation that Russia would rearrange her institutions along the lines of the Western parliamentary model, a useful asset in stressing the aspect of the war as a struggle between liberal democracy and autocratic Central European militarism. It was taken for granted in the West that under her new dispensation Russia would remain in the war, if anything with renewed purpose and vigor. Such was indeed the initial intention of the provisional government, as was made clear by Miliukov, the Foreign Minister.

But in this lay a misunderstanding, no less on the part of the provisional government than of Russia's allies. The weary mass of the Russian people were at this time less interested in the details of constitutional arrangements than in the trinity best summed up in the later slogan, "land, peace, and bread." The first had little to do with the war, expressing as it did a long-existing wish for social reorganization in the Russian state; the other two meant in effect quitting the war. Thus, the March Revolution had the effect of intensifying expectations that it was not capable of satisfying; in this, more than in the details of ineffectual leadership and of specific errors, lay the fundamental vice of its ambiguity. The failure of a last desperate offensive was the turning point. The army literally disintegrated, and many of the soldiers went home to seek land and bread.

In its straits the government had already undergone some changes, out of which emerged in control for a time a Social Revolutionary, Kerensky. Kerensky had abilities of organization and speech, though his personality was not of the strongest and the course of events was escaping his direction. Miliukov had already been jettisoned, and if Russia would not yet advocate peace alone, she espoused the socialist slogan of peace "without annexations or indemnities," while seeking her allies' assent to the same purpose. But there was no possibility of such an agreement being reached, for while Russian events were taking this turn, the other belligerents were in process of surmounting their own individual crises and hence determined to refuse the peace of compromise based on a return to the *status quo ante.*

The Russian situation had therefore to unfold in isolation, its course leading to peace and further revolution. There was in Russia a party prepared for such a radical solution, and in November— October by the old Russian calendar—power fell into its hands. The October Revolution initiated in Russia the still-existing rule of the Bolshevik party.

This outcome, in the circumstances, was a logical one, though it might be more accurate to say that the Bolsheviks seized power than that it fell into their hands. Yet the ease with which they overthrew the existing government must also be remembered. Certainly they had been watching their opportunity, and certainly also there was no dearth of determination and vigor among the Bolshevik leadership.

The name *Bolshevik* is derived from the Russian word for majority, and of majority the Bolsheviks had none in 1917, not even among the followers of Marx, of whom they were a fragment, let alone among the whole Russian people. In proper correspondence with the Marxist view of the course of historic evolution, socialism had had little impact in Russia, whose own evolution had not yet reached the suitable stage of development. Industry and an industrial proletariat had made their appearance in Russia during the two decades before 1914, but they were still small, and for that matter many of the industrial workers were fresh recruits from the land, to which they frequently returned. Moreover, as might be expected, the government of the Tsar had not allowed free scope to socialist agitation, the proponents of which had consequently been driven underground or into exile. Understandably also, in such circumstances, revolution had among Russian socialists a greater appeal than the more evolutionary possibilities that attracted the freely operating socialist parties of the rest of Europe.

These issues used to be debated among Russian socialists, and it was at one of their meetings, in 1903 in London, that the more radical faction secured a temporary majority; thereafter it clung to the appellation, contributing a word to all languages. In this group the figure of Vladimir Ilyich Ulianov, known to history as Lenin, soon rose to a position of prominence and acknowledged leadership. Like virtually all of the early socialist leaders, like Marx himself, Lenin was by background a bourgeois intellectual, endowed with high intelligence and organizing ability, of simple tastes, hard working, ruthless, and a prolific writer. Lenin at the outbreak of war was in Switzerland. Unlike most socialists in the belligerent countries, Lenin had no hesitation in adhering to orthodox Marxist interpretation, and he participated in the previously mentioned meetings that brought together various European socialists in Switzerland. Lenin was very interested in the revolutionary possibilities of the war, which, in keeping with theory, might be expected to find their best prospects in one of the more advanced industrial states. Germany would probably have been the most logical candidate, he thought, but Lenin's predilections in this respect were catholic; he was dedicated to revolution as such—in addition to which war is always full of surprises.

The events of March 1917 in Russia seemed likely to open up unexpected horizons, and Lenin was anxious to return to Russia. The problem of how to effect the transit across belligerent lines was solved for him by the Germans. It was an interesting arrangement, a calculation—or a gamble—wholly logical on both sides; it was also one in which one may see running the long thread of Russo-German common action, at times in the most startling and unexpected circumstances. Ludendorff was no Bolshevik, but his calculation was sound that Lenin would contribute to the increase of Russian chaos, thereby enhancing the German prospects of knocking Russia out of the war, a reverse version of the Schlieffen Plan. If victory could first be secured over Russia, Bolshevism could then be dealt with adequately and at leisure. This Lenin fully understood, but calculated in turn that if revolution could once secure a firm base, from there it might spread, to Germany included, where Ludendorff and his ilk could then be disposed of in suitable manner. In the famous "sealed train" Lenin and some of his followers were conveyed across Germany to Stockholm, whence they went on to Petrograd where Lenin arrived in April 1917.

Lenin was little concerned by the extent of the support, or lack of it, he had in Russia. The bases of his operation were the Soviets, local councils which had already made their appearance in the

Revolution of 1905. Making the most of the peace issue, he broad-
ened his own influence, and simultaneously that of his principal
supporter, the Petrograd Soviet, increasingly a rival to the fumbling
provisional government. Following a false start, a premature attempt in July that was crushed and caused Lenin to seek temporary
shelter in Finland, the Bolsheviks resumed their progress. They had
managed to secure a majority in the Petrograd Soviet, to the chair-
manship of which Trotsky[4] was elected. When Lenin decided the
time was ripe, the final transfer of power was effected with ease.

Here was a new situation indeed, and not least for Lenin and
the Bolsheviks themselves. To agitate for the *tabula rasa* of existing
institutions, as they had so far spent their lives in doing, is one
thing; to operate the power of a state is another. Certain matters,
constitutional ones, were disposed of with simplicity and in radical
fashion. The election of a constitutional assembly, scheduled by the
provisional government, fell due almost immediately after the Bolshevik take-over. As might have been expected, the election produced a large majority for the Social Revolutionaries[5] rather than
for the relatively little-known Bolsheviks. Lenin was not hampered
by scruples; he wasted little time in dismissing the unamenable
assembly shortly after it met in January. Such a turn of events is
not unusual in a revolution. It led in this case to a very important
result: since the Russian people in their mass were not ready, they
would be governed for the time being by the dictatorship of the
proletariat, meaning in fact by a dictatorship of its self-appointed
Bolshevik leaders. The consequences of this early situation may well
be described as incalculable, for it obtains to this day, nearly half
a century later. Power the Bolsheviks would not yield, but proceeded instead to effect the proper education of the Russian people
while—an even more formidable task—seeking to create the bases
of industry and proletariat that theoretically should have anteceded

---

[4] Trotsky, an able and flamboyant personality, had suffered the usual fate of
Russian revolutionaries, imprisonment and exile. He had participated in the
Revolution of 1905, but despite his earlier Menshevik leanings he threw in his
lot with the Bolsheviks, returning to Russia from the United States, where the
outbreak of revolution had found him.
[5] The Social Revolutionaries had sought to adapt Marxist views to Russian conditions, directing their attention to the peasants, among whom they had achieved
considerable success.

revolution. This reversal, or distortion, of the proper historical sequence was one of the unexpected consequences resulting from the accident of war.

The ultimate development of Russia clearly would take a long time, but the immediate fact of war could not wait. With it the Bolsheviks dealt in such a fashion that the Revolution, born of war, was made to have an enormous impact considerably beyond the boundaries of Russia. That the country had collapsed was a fact, the acknowledgment of which led to the logical conclusion that an end must be put to the war. This was precisely the German calculation, and the Germans were anxious to make peace with Russia, but since the Russian collapse represented their victory they felt they could impose their own conditions, which were extraordinarily harsh. Following the conclusion of an armistice in December, negotiations for peace were carried on at Brest-Litovsk. The German demands were such as to cause even some of the Bolsheviks to recoil, but Lenin's ruthless logic carried the day: what mattered territorial losses, or any other demands, when all would soon be undone by the looming world revolution? Peace was accordingly signed in March. The Treaty of Brest-Litovsk deprived Russia of all her non-Russian acquisitions in Europe since the eighteenth century, while the Ukraine, from whose food resources the Germans had great hopes, was dealt with as a separate entity.

Important as these things in some respects were, we may agree with Lenin's view at the time that they were of only secondary significance. The same view may even be taken of the civil war, or wars, into which Russia was plunged as an aftermath of the Revolution. These struggles continued for more than three years, causing far greater havoc and misery than had the war just concluded. They led to a variety of complications, foreign among others, and had very important effects on the internal course of Russian developments. With all this we are not now concerned, but rather with the fact that the Revolution was saved, Bolshevik control confirmed and even strengthened, and with it the other aspect of Bolshevik strategy for dealing with the war in which the rest of the belligerents were still locked.

Lenin's great purpose, we have seen, was not so much revolution

in Russia—this could be a useful, if adventitious, accident—as the
transformation on a universal, or at least a European, scale of the
war among states into war between classes—in brief, world revolution. He was in fact convinced at first that unless this occurred the
outside world somehow would crush the Revolution in Russia. With
complete impartiality therefore, making no distinction between ex-
friend and ex-foe, the Bolsheviks appealed to the proletarians everywhere to follow their example. That the Russian events should
elicit interest and response among socialists outside of Russia is the
least that could be expected; even the tamer elements that had
become reconciled to the hope of orderly parliamentary processes
could not but be impressed by the fact that here was a state where
Marx had taken over. This must be seen, besides, in the previously
mentioned context of war weariness, more limitedly in that of the
revival of a critical socialist attitude everywhere.

The governments of the belligerents had more than ever legitimate cause for concern, and some of them, the British and the
French, for instance, impeded the participation of their own socialists in the meeting that took place in Stockholm in September 1917.
That gathering, though inconclusive, was a reflection of the Russian
events by which it was dominated. It had grown out of a Dutch
initiative to which the Menshevik-dominated Petrograd Soviet had
responded, but the Bolsheviks were no more enthusiastic about it
than were some of the other suspicious governments. The limited
socialist representation that finally met in Stockholm accomplished
little; the leadership of the radical Left was passing into the hands
of the Bolsheviks on an international scale, though it would take
some further time before they would launch the Third, or Communist, International[6] and the split between Communist and Socialist would become irrevocably formalized.

Nevertheless, at the grass roots of socialism especially, there was
considerable interest, albeit accompanied by little concrete knowledge, in what was going on in Russia, and the moderate socialist
leadership had some difficulty in holding its own forces in line.

---

[6] The Third, or Communist, International, the Comintern, was organized in
1919, like its predecessor for the purpose of coordinating the workers' movement
in the various national units. The fact of Communist control in Russia naturally
gave the Russian leadership a prominent, not to say a totally dominant, position
in the Comintern.

Mention has been made of the strikes that occurred in 1917; it was in that year, after some murderously futile offensives, that there were mutinies in the French army. The wearisome and dangerous passage was overcome, thanks in large measure to the humane and skillful action of General Pétain, who insisted, however, that for the coming year the French could do no more than hold and wait. The French situation was a very difficult one throughout the major part of the year; it found reflection in parliamentary restlessness and changes in the government (participation in which the Socialist party abandoned) and was not resolved until the advent to the Prime Ministership in November of Clemenceau, who was to do for France what Lloyd George had for a year been doing for England.

Across the Rhine it was in July of the same year that the famous "peace resolution," vague as it was, nevertheless obtained a majority in the Reichstag. But the collapse of Russia revived German hopes of victory, and the peace resolution was forgotten even by some of its proponents. A struggle had been going on in Germany between the military and the government, in which the former emerged triumphant. The Chancellor, Bethmann-Hollweg, had been opposed to the adoption of unrestricted submarine warfare and was in favor of domestic reforms, such as suffrage concessions, in order to appease the discontent of socialist-oriented workers. He was even not opposed to exploring the possibilities of a peace of compromise. His hedging tactics brought about a showdown with the military, Hindenburg and Ludendorff threatening to resign. Finding no longer support in any quarters, he himself finally resigned in July. His successor, Michaelis, was an even weaker man, whose accession to office signalized the complete success of the military. Even the Kaiser's role was increasingly one of effacement, and we may fairly speak thereafter of military dictatorship in Germany.

The elimination of Russia from the war was obviously a disaster of the first magnitude for the Allies, occurring as it did at a time of uncertain morale, to the further lowering of which it contributed heavily. German hopes were in fact not wholly devoid of foundation, and it might have gone ill for the Allies had they not, at the same time that Russia was defecting, received the assurance of additional help from a different quarter. It is a highly interesting coincidence that the Russian Revolution and the American intervention should have been virtually simultaneous. Both were events that grew out of the European war. They involved in the affairs of Europe a country that was definitely not European and one that was of Europe yet on the margin of it. It is by now an obvious platitude to say that it is proper to see in these two happenings the deepest significance of the war as well as an expression of historical continuity. The Russian Revolution was the accident of war that had brought about the success of the long-familiar Marxist idea, henceforth to be held up as a beacon by Russia. The democratic idea is older than the Marxist; it was in many ways wholly suitable that it should fall to the United States to be its chief exponent and defender.

The Democratic Answer

What happened in March and April of 1917 was destined to alter completely the nature of the war. Hitherto the war could be looked upon as an episode in the traditional contest among the powers of Europe. Even if one grants that a victory of the Central Powers would have gone a long distance toward establishing a German hegemony, hence viewing the war in a broad sense as a German bid for the accomplishment of that purpose, reminiscent to a degree of the Napoleonic, then the Allies were fighting primarily for the prevention of such an outcome, the preservation of the classical balance of power. Within this purpose, they hoped to secure for themselves certain specified advantages; we have seen the concrete manifestations of their attempt to do this in what may be described as the diplomacy of power, registered in the various agreements contrived by the Allies among themselves.

There was much in these understandings that would have had but meager appeal to their peoples, and some stress had been placed on the ideological aspect of the struggle, an attempt hampered by the autocratic nature of the government of the Tsar. This was changed by the March Revolution in Russia, which is why Russia's allies welcomed it at first. Despite a second revolution, Russia, though defeated and impotent, remained an ever-present factor in all calculations, not only as a sovereign state, but because she now stood in the eyes of all as the standard-bearer of an idea.

Within a month of the first revolution in Petrograd the United States declared war upon Germany. This was, in military terms, extremely important, but more important still was the fact that American intervention shifted the emphasis of the war away from the aspect of a traditional competition for power toward that of an ideological contest. There is in such a contest at once higher hope and greater danger.

For a time the Allied coalition could indeed describe itself as a coalition of the democracies, and it was wholly appropriate that in his war message to the Congress President Wilson should have referred to the Russian Revolution in these words: "Does not every American feel that assurance has been added to our hope for the future peace of the world by the wonderful and heartening things that have been happening within the last few weeks in Russia?" The transformation of momentary agreement into a rivalry unreconciled to this day is as important as any of the long-term consequences of the First World War.

The American intervention and the reasons for it may be dealt with very briefly. In the immediate and narrow sense the precipitating issue was submarine warfare. The law of the seas as it existed contained many curious provisions and had failed to secure wide international recognition. There were nevertheless some well-established understandings about the rights of neutrals in wartime, matters having to do with such things as blockade, trade, and contraband. Such as they were, these understandings had grown up at a time when maritime activity was on the surface of the water. The submarine was in 1914 a relatively novel device, the use and importance of which was a by-product of the war itself. Its very nature made it unsuited to abide by the laws of war at sea, thus placing its would-be user at a moral disadvantage. That user would naturally be Germany, which might hope in this fashion to compensate for the inferiority of her surface fleet. Germany therefore found herself in a situation comparable to that with which Belgian neutrality confronted her: her plighted word stood in the way of her desires. She dealt with the two situations in similar fashion, asserting the higher law of necessity.

Interfering with the traffic of neutrals at sea had given rise to early contentions between belligerents and neutrals, among whom the United States was far the most important, but clearly, interference with the rights of property alone is less serious than the same interference compounded by the loss of life. The sinking of the *Lusitania* was a sensational event, and in 1915 Germany had consented to relent in the application of submarine warfare. But as the war went on and victory seemed forever elusive, the question was considered again in Germany whether in the now perfected underwater craft might not lie the key to its achievement. Britain was highly vulnerable and far more susceptible than any other power to the consequences of an effective blockade. In January 1917 Germany made the decision to resort to unrestricted submarine warfare.

The decision had been carefully weighed and debated, and there were no illusions in Germany about its probable impact on the American position. The same considerations prevailed as in the Belgian case, the time factor for one: the outcome would be settled before unready America could act, and the same submarine would prevent in addition the conveyance to Europe of any effective American assistance. The debate between America and Germany was brief and was resolved with the American declaration of war in April.

All this is simple and clear, as well as incontrovertible. But there was more to it. Even apart from closer ideological affinity with the Western democracies, not to mention the fact of America's British cultural heritage, the circumstances of the war had the effect of creating concrete links of interest between America and the Allies: industry, agriculture, trade, finance were all involved, while contact with the Central Powers was largely severed. Still more important, though more elusive and less sharply perceived at the time, was the larger consideration of the long-term national interest. Just as the tacit but effective nineteenth-century role of British power in shielding America had been of the utmost significance, might not the unwritten identity of British and American interest extend to the point where the traditional British defense of the European balance of power—Britain's chief purpose in the current war as in others—had become an American interest as well? Put it another way, was a German-dominated Europe desirable from the American point of view, and if not, how much should be done to prevent such an outcome? Colonel House's awareness of this possibility has been mentioned, which did not blind him, however, to the converse prospect of too great Russian enhancement. It was particularly fortunate that in March 1917 Russia should have had a revolution, though an immediate causal connection between that event and the subsequent American declaration of war would indeed be far to seek. Nevertheless, the above considerations are highly germane to the future course of developments.

The American contribution to the war was ultimately decisive and, from the point of view of the Allies, may be described as the exchange of Russia for America, a most profitable operation indeed. In military terms, especially on land, America could at first offer little, but even apart from the highly important fact that the American intervention solved some awkward problems of supplies and financing, the knowledge that the virtually unlimited reservoir of American resources was now enlisted in the Allied cause was an enormous boost to morale. If only the Allies could hold on for the moment, they could feel confident of the ultimate outcome. Conversely, unless Germany could bring the war to a rapid and successful conclusion, there was no hope for her. This, in brief, is the story of the end of the war: the continuing drain of irreplaceable resources on one side, their mounting accumulation on the other, until the scales of victory were tipped. This was important enough, especially for what it meant in long-term rearrangements of power, a consideration to which we shall return; but for the more immediate future the impact of the American intervention was more marked in another domain.

In 1917 America was relatively unknown to Europe, more a land of myth than of reality, and if there was greater American knowledge of Europe there was also deep American consciousness of difference. In this respect the American President was an authentic representative of his people; the fact is significant that in the newly formed coalition America never became formally an ally, retaining instead the status of "associated" power. In this there was some danger that distinctness might become translated—as to a point it was—into a feeling of moral superiority. Yet the basis of distinction was authentic. The quarrels of Europe, in the sense that they had precipitated the war, had virtually no echo in America, and if the balance of power might be a desirable condition even for America, the detailed implementation of it could take different forms in American and in European eyes. In this respect America stood nearest Britain, though the British participation in the more sordid aspects of imperial barterings, for example, was alien to the American approach. Certainly America was innocent of participation in the network of inter-Allied arrangements registered in the series of secret treaties mentioned before. Put another way, America's hands were clean. While this is simple fact, it does not on the other hand mean that American man is or was fundamentally different from others, or that there is any warrant for translating different circumstances, historical in part, into some such feeling as "I thank thee, Lord, that I am not like unto other men." The accusation of cant—it has been made, and quite understandably—has often been directed at America.

In terms of constitutional arrangements America was older than most European states, but the revolutionary origins of America could strike, and still do, a responsive chord among the American people. That is why the Revolution in Russia could be welcome, as representing nothing more than the introduction to the advantages of the more advanced stage of development that America had long known. In any case, the unique position of the United States, be it in terms of power or of the place it held among the belligerents, made America the logical spokesman of the Allied cause. Since the United States was seeking no material gain and had no deep consciousness of threat to its own position, it could hardly do otherwise than stress the ideological aspect of the war. The undesirability of Prussian militarism could be accepted, but America had no quarrel with the German people as such, only with their government and its cynical, law-breaking methods. The eighteenth-century belief in the fundamental goodness of man was still an active component of the American ethos; let the German people, and others, espouse democracy, and the threat of irresponsible aggression would disappear. Law, as derived from the will of the people, was the way to the good society and an orderly community of states; "to make the world safe for democracy" was the cure to the world's current ills. All this was hardly new, and to our disillusioned age much of it may seem steeped in naïveté; yet it must be borne in mind that here was potent medicine, the summation of hopes that had inspired much of the nineteenth-century political struggle. The right of peoples to decide the nature of their governments as well as of their national allegiance had in Europe received its chief impulse from the French Revolution. The circumstances of the time made America—powerful, uncommitted to secret bargains, untried so far by the ordeal of war—the best qualified to stand for these ideals with authority. And the American President was not in the least loath to assume the role of world leader.

Slogans are useful things in battle and as general expressions of national purpose. But their vagueness will hardly suffice for the operation of states or foreign offices until they are made more concrete in formulation. The American government, Wilson included, was not a collectivity of starry-eyed innocents but a gathering of men well aware of reality, however high their purpose. They knew, for example, that the application of the principle of self-determination would mean alterations in the map of Europe, to say nothing of the troublesome fact that the precise determination of national allegiance is not always the simple matter that it may at first glance appear to be.

Reliable, unbiased information was needed that was not at Wilson's own command. He did the obvious thing. In order to prepare concrete plans for the peace, Wilson and his confidant, House, relied on the work of *The Inquiry*. This was the name informally adopted to designate the collection of technicians in a variety of fields— history, law, geography, ethnology, and others—experts, as the word went, whose task it was to prepare reports and memoranda on a multitude of specific situations. This they did, and their work was of high quality; there was no dearth of technical competence in America, the legend of whose innocence in this respect is pure myth.

This is the origin of the Fourteen Points, in large measure abstracted from the comprehensive report of the "experts." The program for the future—for peace in the immediate sense, but beyond that for the organization of an orderly, rational world—was announced to the American people in a speech that Wilson delivered before the Congress on January 8, 1918. The importance of this historic document, at the time and since, can hardly be overemphasized; for that reason, familiar as the Fourteen Points may be, they warrant being quoted in full.

I. Open covenants of peace openly arrived at, after which there shall be no private international understandings of any kind, but diplomacy shall proceed always frankly and in the public view.

II. Absolute freedom of navigation upon the seas outside territorial waters alike in peace and in war, except as the seas may be closed in whole or in part by international action or the enforcement of international covenants.

III. The removal, so far as possible, of all economic barriers and the establishment of an equality of trade conditions among all the nations consenting to the peace and associating themselves for its maintenance.

IV. Adequate guarantees given and taken that national armaments will be reduced to the lowest point consistent with domestic safety.

V. A free, open-minded and absolutely impartial adjustment of all colonial claims based upon a strict observance of the principle that in determining all such questions of sovereignty the interests of the populations concerned must have equal weight with the equitable claims of the government whose title is to be determined.

VI. The evacuation of all Russian territory, and such a settlement of all questions affecting Russia as will secure the best and freest cooperation of the other nations of the world in obtaining for her an unhampered and unembarrassed opportunity for the independent determination of her own political development and national policy, and assure her of a sincere welcome into the society of free nations under institutions of her own choosing; and, more than a welcome, assistance also of every kind that she may need and may herself desire. The treatment accorded Russia by her sister nations in the months to come will be the acid test of their good-will, of their comprehension of her needs as disintinguished from their own interests, and of their intelligent and unselfish sympathy.

VII. Belgium, the whole world will agree must be evacuated and restored, without any attempt to limit the sovereignty which she enjoys in common with all other free nations. No other single act will serve to restore confidence among the nations in the laws which they have themselves set and determined for the government of their relations with one another. Without this healing act the whole structure and validity of international law is forever impaired.

VIII. All French territory should be freed and the invaded portions restored, and the wrong done to France by Prussia in 1871 in the matter of Alsace-Lorraine, which has unsettled the peace of the world for nearly fifty years, should be righted, in order that peace may once more be made secure in the interest of all.

IX. A readjustment of the frontiers of Italy should be effected along clearly recognizable lines of nationality.

X. The peoples of Austria-Hungary, whose place among the nations we wish to see safeguarded and assured, should be accorded the freest opportunity of autonomous development.

XI. Rumania, Serbia and Montenegro should be evacuated; occupied territories restored; Serbia accorded free and secure access to the sea; and the relations of the several Balkan states to one another determined by friendly counsel along historically established lines of allegiance and nationality; and international guarantees of the political and economic independence and territorial integrity of the several Balkan states should be entered upon.

XII. The Turkish portions of the present Ottoman Empire should be assured a secure sovereignty, but the other nationalities which are now under Turkish rule should be assured an undoubted security of life and an absolutely unmolested opportunity of autonomous development, and the Dardanelles should be permanently opened as a free passage to the ships and commerce of all nations under international guarantees.

XIII. An independent Polish State should be erected which should include the territories inhabited by indisputably Polish populations, which should be assured a free and secure access to the sea, and whose political and economic independence and territorial integrity should be guaranteed by international covenant.

XIV. A general association of nations must be formed under specific covenants for the purpose of affording mutual guarantees of political independence and territorial integrity to great and small States alike.

This program clearly contains two types of provisions. The major part of the Fourteen Points dealt with specific questions (Alsace-Lorraine, Poland, the Balkans, etc.), in all cases endorsing the principle of self-determination. There were, in addition, some declarations of general principle, of which the most significant are the first and the last: Point I was a condemnation of the traditional secret ways of diplomacy, the arranging of the fate of peoples without their knowledge or consent, and advocated instead "open covenants, openly arrived at." The Fourteenth Point proposed the establishment of an international organization, the main function of which would be the preservation of peace, transferring to the international level the maintenance of order under the rule of law that characterized the domestic operation of the civilized modern state. This last point may be regarded as Wilson's own, his special and most cherished contribution.

Yet none of this was actually new, not even the advocacy of an international organization, for the prospect of establishing a rule of law among states had long occupied the minds of thinking men. What the American President was doing was no more than endorsing the forces of history, especially the nineteenth-century trends of democracy and of nationalism, twin facets of the basic assertion of the Rights of Man. This was the direction of progress, endowed with the moral attribute of good, and it expressed an optimistic view of history that befitted the young, vigorous, and successful entity that was the United States. It was of the highest significance, however, that the most powerful state in the world should put the weight of its influence behind such a program; it should be recalled that a not very different program announced by Lloyd George three days earlier has received from history but relatively scant attention. The overwhelming power and the unique position, in moral terms, of the United States was unquestioningly acknowledged by all.

The Wilsonian program attracted wide attention. It was not difficult for the Allies to give it their endorsement; apart from the fact that no one will publicly favor sin, they generally stood to benefit from the application of the principle of self-determination, which in fact they themselves had been advocating. It was otherwise with the Central Powers; at the government level their response was nonexistent. At the beginning of 1918 hopes of victory were still nourished by the German command. If the Russian collapse had not brought in its train all the benefits that had been hoped for— in particular, the Ukrainian granary was disappointing—it had made possible a large concentration of forces on the Western front, henceforth the decisive theater of war. The offensives that Ludendorff was able to mount in the spring of 1918 gave the Allies serious concern, to the extent indeed of inducing them at last to unite their forces under a single command. But the French had been able to rest and recover, the effects of conscription had increased the size of the British contingent, and, most of all, the submarine had failed to interfere with the flow of American assistance in either goods or men; nearly two million Americans had safely crossed the Atlantic, and some of them had begun to appear at the front.

The end came quickly. By August Germany had played her last card, she had exhausted her reserves, and a steady, though orderly, retreat began. Simultaneously, the Balkan front came to life, and the first sign of formal collapse appeared in Bulgaria, which concluded an armistice at the end of September. A month later the Ottoman Empire followed suit, then Austria-Hungary a few days later, after the Italians had begun to move. The active phase of the war came to an end with the cessation of fighting on the Western front on November 11. Of the events that occurred during the last two months of the war, certain things are especially relevant to the present discussion.

Developments in Russia were relatively little affected by the end of the war. Needless to say, the Central Powers had to withdraw from the area, though it took some time and some difficulty to induce them to do this, but Russia was still faced with civil war and the emergence of liberated peoples on her former western borders. To a considerable extent, matters in Eastern Europe were outside the control of the Allies, and confusion continued to reign in that quarter for some time. The case of Austria-Hungary can only be described as one of internal disintegration. The belated attempts of Charles I to reorganize the ramshackle structure of the state were unavailing in the face of defeat; in Prague, in Budapest, in Vienna, in Zagreb, national independence was proclaimed while various Allied forces were advancing from the west and the south. Here was a multitude of problems in the making that the peace would have to endeavor to settle.

But the most significant developments were those that took place in connection with the conclusion of the German armistice. These occurred at two distinct but closely related levels. When Ludendorff lost his nerve and came to the conclusion that the war could not be won, the German command, rational men that they were, drew from this the further conclusion that an end must be put to the fighting. Fearing that retreat might turn into a rout, in somewhat humorless —or perhaps humorous—fashion they "discovered" the civilian government, whose task—not theirs—it was to extricate Germany from her predicament. It was at this point that the merits of the Fourteen Points (was not the concept of a "just" rather than a punitive peace at the heart of that program?) were discovered in Germany. Consequently, the German government addressed itself to the American with a request for an armistice preliminary to peace on the basis of the American proposals.

The exchanges that took place between the German and the American governments emphasized the distinction between the German people and their leaders. This had the effect of encouraging the forces of change in Germany, where the Socialists were already participating in the government. October and early November were a trying time in Germany, where the tragedy of defeat unfolded its last act. Ludendorff was displaced, and the Kaiser himself, in face of the mood of his people and of some disaffection among the armed forces, abdicated and fled to Holland.

In Berlin, the fact of abdication was preceded by the announcement of it by the Chancellor, and on November 9 the Socialist Party leader, Scheidemann, proclaimed the Republic. Considering the circumstances, the revolutionary transition was surprisingly smooth, unaccompanied by bloodshed. Considerable significance attaches to this, no less than to the fact that the Socialists, and the forces of the Left in general, by accepting the responsibility of power, found themselves saddled with responsibility for the fate of the country. This meant the preservation of order, hence the suppression of the more radical revolutionary tendencies on the one hand, the formal act of surrender on the other.

The American "associate" was not formally empowered to speak for the Allies; it could therefore do no other than consult them before replying to the German request. This it did, and for a few days a crucial, close, and at times difficult discussion took place between the Allied representatives and Colonel House. Whatever lack of clarity there may have been in the Fourteen Points was removed on this occasion, the outcome of which was almost unqualified acceptance of the program by the Allies.[7] On the basis of this understanding a military armistice was negotiated and came into force. It might be mentioned in passing that the terms of the armistice were tantamount to unconditional surrender—Germany had no choice, being defeated—but that this is also the situation which later on, when the peace came to be much criticized, gave rise to the legend that Germany had not really been defeated but had instead been tricked into surrender by promises that subsequently were broken. The consequences of this ambiguity were eventually very considerable, but this is not the place to dwell on them.

The war came to an end with total Allied victory. Of their own volition, or perhaps one should say more accurately under the prodding of American pressure, all had committed themselves to a definite program for the shape of the peace.

[7] An elaborate gloss on the Fourteen Points had been prepared with a view to making wholly clear and specific their content and their meaning. What reservations were finally made by the Allies, save in the Italian case which did not affect the German aspect of the situation, were relatively insignificant.

4

The War's End: The Climate of Expectations

The popular tendency is strong to equate the absence or the cessation of fighting with the existence of peace. But the transition twilight passage from the one condition to the other is one of great importance and is strewn with many shoals. Considering the multitude of concrete issues that had to be resolved in 1918, under the best of circumstances and with the best of will and luck it would take considerable time before the formal terms of peace could be elaborated.

Preparations for the peace had long been in the making. The American program has been mentioned; the British and the French had similarly given much thought to the future, not to mention the various agreements into which they had already entered. It took barely more than two months before the peace congress formally opened in Paris; this may seem to us very expeditious procedure, but in 1918 there were complaints of dilatoriness. We may pause briefly to take stock of the climate, of the state of the world, at the close of 1918.

Certain important things had happened. One of these was the American election that took place at the very moment when the last armistice was being concluded. The Presidential office was not at stake, but Wilson's appeal for a Democratic Congress was misread and backfired. The operation of American constitutional arrangements produced on this occasion a balance of power with a vengeance, the consequences of which some have regarded as disastrous. Wilson's subsequent failure to allow any scope for Republican representation on the American peace delegation must be seen as an unperceptive blunder.

The personality of Woodrow Wilson—he has been called the Fifteenth Point—is a matter of no little importance. The task ahead of him he found elating, and there is no question that his purpose was high; justice, democracy, and peace he would help enthrone in the world. As he put it to the American delegates on board the *George Washington* on the passage to Europe, "Tell me what's right, and I'll fight for it." This is fair summation of his own approach. Yet the fact that he had decided to lead that delegation in person was a measure of the degree of his distrust of others; no one but he could be entrusted with the task of fighting with sufficient resolution. True American that he was, his confidence in the leaders of Europe was qualified, nor was his temperament devoid of certain autocratic tendencies, of that difficulty in getting along with individual representatives of the species so often found in would-be reforming lovers of mankind. Divergence of opinion, even if honestly founded and meant, he tended to equate with the difference between wrong and right, evil and good.

If not the suspicion, then at least the awareness of difference with Europeans was in large measure justified. For there was indeed a great difference between the historical experiences, both older and more recent ones, of America and of Europe. Aged, hard-bitten Clemenceau, France's "father of victory," was a sincere French patriot above all; he understood power in the Bismarckian fashion, and for all his authentic Jacobin derivation, he spoke of Wilson's dream as "noble candor." Lloyd George was more supple and mercurial, as well as less reliably predictable. He too understood power, not least in the domestic domain. Lloyd George thought to capitalize on the elation of victory by holding an election in December. The British electorate in 1918 behaved differently from that of 1945; Lloyd George's calculations proved correct, at least in the immediate and limited sense, for he handsomely won the "khaki" election. It was the same Lloyd George who was responsible for the phrase "a world fit for heroes to live in." Our more disillusioned age might prefer the more homely "pie in the sky" description, expressive of unattainability. But this is precisely the point on which our ages differ; the climate of expectations was enormously high in 1918.

Weariness and revulsion from war had made a deep impression on all the European belligerents; these feelings were reflected in combined restlessness and hope. Much was heard of the phrase "the war to end all wars"; the blood bath of four years must not happen again. By contrast, the war had affected America but little. It had meant profit and accelerated economic growth, and to the drafted men quite often little more than a fairly pleasant voyage abroad. American casualties were, in comparative terms, insignificant. The American experience in its totality belied the view that there are no benefits in war. Consequently, there was no reason for America's optimism in the future to be qualified, as it was for Europeans, by the sensation of fatigue resulting from too great an effort and from mournings over mountains of dead and hordes of disabled. It was entirely appropriate that the New World should be the active bearer of the hopes of mankind and that from it should have come the Messiah of a bright New Order.

Wilson was conscious of this and in his own person received the deep homage to the high standing that was America's for a brief time. The authentic enthusiasm with which the masses greeted him everywhere he went was clear expression of this, calculated to induce in him the dangerous feeling that he was a more authentic spokesman of their hopes than were their own national representatives. The feeling was not wholly unjustified; America had been the savior, and that role she would now continue to perform by bringing peace that would be lasting because it was based on justice. Simple ideas and slogans, oversimplified ones indeed, will elicit a ready response from the mass. From the multiplicity that is man the good as well as the evil side of his nature can easily be made to respond. Great events like the war, that shake loose the drab sordidness of daily routine, are calculated to release man's great potentialities for the best as well as for the worst.

Even the defeated enemy could respond to the appeal of peace founded on justice. But it is precisely at this point that the ambivalence and ambiguity contained in simple slogans could intrude. For the war had also served to exacerbate passions, the nationalistic most of all. The German people felt no guilt for what had happened, and in so far as they might grant that their government had been tainted by the lack of democratic virtue, had they not made amends with their revolution that had rid them of the Kaiser and put power in the hands of the people? Had not the American President for that matter proclaimed that he had no quarrel with the German people, but only with their governmental system? Justice, for the German people, must be divorced from punitive retribution.

But retribution was precisely what justice meant for the Allies. In addition to the slogan "Hang the Kaiser!" the British used in their election another one, "Squeeze Germany until the pips squeak." The French could not bring back to life their dead, but apart from taking for granted the righting of the wrong of 1871— even the Fourteen Points had specified this—they had no doubt that they had been the victims of aggression, and it was an undeniable fact that they had furnished the chief battleground of the war. Thus it was clearly no more than the simplest implementation of justice that the colossal damage should be made good by the aggressor; quite properly, the Fourteen Points had mentioned this too. There is little question that at the end of 1918 nationalistic emotion ran high.

Matters were somewhat different in Central Europe and in the East. Nationalism was intense in the fragments of what had been Austria-Hungary, the destruction of which was in fact the highest tribute to the nationalistic idea. In mid-Europe it was in large measure a question of organizing new entities. This at once raised the question, harbinger of a host of future problems, of precisely where the frontiers of each new national entity should be. Just because these nationalities considered themselves to have been victims of oppression, their common tendency was to be suspicious, aggressive, and intolerant rather than the reverse. Administrations were improvised in great haste, plans for constitutions—democratic of course—were made, and new national armies began to appear.

Russia was a different case. The Bolshevik leadership professed little concern with nationalism but was involved instead in the elementary struggle for survival, all the while hoping to spread the new gospel abroad. Strong as nationalism may have been elsewhere, many eyes were turned in fascination toward the Russian experiment. The Marxist ideology, long familiar to many, put stress on justice too, but at the social rather than at the national level. High as was the prestige of democracy, how much and how fast could democracy give satisfaction to the social discontent of the masses, of which there was so much abroad? In a sense, America and Russia were competing exponents of hope, between whom there was, in the last analysis, much common ground. As it has been expressed, with justice, Wilson and Lenin stood before the world as rival prophets.

But it must be stressed again that as the concrete task of making peace was about to begin, Europe stood poised in suspicious unrest combined with highest hope. Just because the expectations were so high, the task of satisfying them, while reconciling the exacerbated feelings to which the war itself had contributed much, was perhaps —not very surprisingly in retrospect—beyond the capacity of the would-be peacemakers.

The Peace, An Impossible Task

1

The Settlements That Issued from the War

By mid-January 1919 preparations had been completed. Representatives of nearly all nations were assembled in Paris for the purpose of putting together again in some viable order the pieces of a world that had exploded five years earlier. The task was clearly of enormous magnitude, by contrast with which that of the Vienna Congress, the example most comparable, paled into insignificance. The world of 1919 was infinitely more complex than that of 1814, be it on the score of the intricate multiplicity of its economic connections, or because of the pressure of the masses clamoring for recognition. These were the great nineteenth-century contributions.

How to operate under these circumstances was itself no small issue. The peoples were ostensibly represented by their legitimately constituted delegates, but clearly there could be little question of functioning in parliamentary guise; with power went responsibility, and very early power came to be concentrated to a remarkable degree in few hands. The Supreme War Council, central directing agency of the Allied war effort, became the Supreme Council, directing agency of the peacemaking, and very soon five men, the heads of delegations of the five great powers, took into their own hands the shaping of the peace. But these men did not have, as indeed they could not, the detailed competence for dealing with a host of matters that called for technical knowledge. The consequence was inescapable: committees of "experts" were appointed to deal with most of these problems, and to a large extent their recommendations were embodied into the final texts of the treaties of peace. For the most part this was highly competent work. The court of last resort, the Supreme Council, the Big Five, retained of course the right of ultimate decision and also reserved for itself the right of dealing with certain essentially political issues.

Of the Five, one, the Japanese member, played but an insignificant role, for the reason that the problems of the peace were predominantly European. Of the remaining Four, the Italian also played but a minor part save where narrowly provincial Italian interests were involved. Germany was to an overwhelming degree the focus of attention in Paris. The peace therefore was primarily the work of three states—the United States, Great Britain, and France—mainly concerned with a fourth—Germany. The war had truly been a manifestation of the German problem. One might even say that the peace was the work of three men, since theirs was the ultimate responsibility of decision. Of Wilson, Lloyd George, and Clemenceau something has already been said: their highly contrasting personalities, their different backgrounds, and the divergence of the interests which it was their proper function to defend, are a very important aspect of the peacemaking. The fourth, the Italian Orlando, personally perhaps the most agreeable, was also the weakest, representing the weakest power among the Four.

Partly because of the experience of Vienna a hundred years before, Germany was essentially excluded from the drafting of the peace. Talleyrand's role and success were well remembered. In such a situation as had existed at Vienna and now obtained in Paris, obviously the best, if not the only, tool of the impotent enemy lies in exploiting dissensions among the victorious coalition, usually not too difficult a task. The fact of victory itself dissolves the most solid cement of a coalition, and the Allies were fully aware of their differences, that there was no need of external intrusion to exacerbate. After they had resolved these differences, a German delegation was invited to Paris, in May, but the observations that it was allowed to make received little attention. The contention therefore that the Treaty of Versailles was an imposed settlement, a *diktat* if one will, is justified; how relevant the fact, and how fair the treaty, are entirely different matters, to which we shall return presently.

The initial awareness of the magnitude of the task had created in turn the decisive need for adequate time. The original intention had been to make a quick preliminary peace, the detailed provisions of which could then be elaborated at leisure. But as it happened, the work proceeded with such celerity that it was found in May that enough had been done to formulate the terms of final peace with Germany. The Treaty of Versailles was signed on June 28; with deliberate pomp and circumstance, in the very setting where the birth of the German Empire had been proclaimed, its demise was registered. Symbolically, as well as in fact, the "wrong" of 1871 had been undone.

The German Peace

The widespread identification of the entire work of the peace conference of Paris with the Treaty of Versailles is incorrect. Versailles dealt with Germany alone, and there were many problems besides that of Germany to settle. Nevertheless it is true, and must be emphasized again, that in 1919 in Paris, just as before 1914, Germany was the prime focus of attention, perhaps to an undue extent.

Certain aspects of the German settlement were relatively simple. That of the frontiers, for example. The application of the principle of nationality could only mean that France would recover Alsace-Lorraine, that Polish territory would be lost, and that the "forgotten" plebiscite that was to have taken place in Schleswig after the wars with Denmark and with Austria might now be held. This is what happened. The French case was very simple—restoration of the frontier of 1870; so was the Danish, a relatively small issue for that matter; the Polish was more difficult because of the passage of time since the eighteenth-century partitions of Poland. A committee was appointed for Poland, and some heated discussions took place; but the latest census—the German one of 1910, be it noted—was essentially the basis of decision. In a zone of mixed population, a Polish majority could enclose an appreciable German minority. This left two moot points, Danzig and Upper Silesia. In the case of the former, Poland's outlet to the sea but a German city, a compromise was effected that created the Free Territory of Danzig, the care of which would be in the hands of the League of Nations. Upper Silesia was not settled until 1922, as the result of a plebiscite; instead of being treated on the basis of a majority for the whole, the territory was partitioned along lines of ethnic division, raising some interesting questions about the nature, the meaning, and the usefulness of plebiscites.

The new Austria was ethnically wholly Germanic, and there was also a compact block of Germans inside the traditional borders of the Kingdom of Bohemia. But the southern frontier of Germany was left unaltered. Historic and strategic considerations were adduced, among others, for retaining these boundaries, considerations whose validity and relevance take on varying weight in different circumstances. In 1919 a hard war had just been fought in which German power had shown itself to be very impressive. This last consideration loomed large in the eyes of the peacemakers, the French most of all. The French felt that their victory would be hollow unless future guarantees were provided against a possible recurrence of German aggression; now was the time to take such reinsurance. Rather than feeling confidence and elation, the French were obsessed by fear for their security. Clemenceau's appraisal was entirely correct that France had been very fortunate in being a member of so powerful a coalition. The permanence of such conditions could hardly be counted on, and the present advantage must be capitalized upon. The attempt to do this took two forms.

The more immediate and concrete was to push Germany back, beyond the Rhine. But the intervening left bank of that river was unquestionably German, and to sever that territory from Germany would have been a clear violation of the principle of self-determination, the creation of an Alsace-Lorraine in reverse. There was close and heated discussion, even high words between Wilson and Clemenceau, but the former was adamant and would not entertain the possibility of a permanent French establishment on the Rhine. America was powerful and Clemenceau was a realist. He therefore yielded, but not until a compromise had been arranged: in recognition of the legitimate French desire for security, America and Britain would commit themselves to assist France against future

German aggression.[1] This major crisis having been overcome, it was possible to deal with another aspect of the matter, compensation for the damage of war.

The reparations chapter is one of the most interesting and strange aspects of the peace. The levying of indemnity on the defeated had been a fairly normal concomitant of war, as the Franco-Prussian War itself had illustrated. This approach has the merit of clarity in its foundation, but the world of 1919 was to be a new and a better world, where justice took the place of retribution based on power. The outcome was that Germany was made liable for the damage of war not because she had been defeated but because she had been the aggressor. Thus, the Treaty of Versailles contains a section entitled "Reparation"—Reparation be it noted, not indemnity—which opens with the since famous so-called war guilt clause:

> The Allied and Associated Governments affirm and Germany accepts the responsibility of Germany and her allies for causing all the loss and damage to which the Allied and Associated Governments and their nationals have been subjected as a consequence of the war imposed upon them by the aggression of Germany and her allies.

Here was Pandora's box, out of which was destined to emerge much evil, untold confusion, and a library of serious historical works, supplemented by a flourishing and vast polemic. The point is not whether, historically and politically, the moral judgment was right or wrong but rather that a moral judgment was introduced into a treaty of peace. To dismiss the attempt as mere puritanical cant—it did appeal more to Wilson than to Clemenceau—would be grossly to misjudge its intent. Just because the connection between power and ethics, between politics and morality, is one fraught with difficulties and dangers is no reason for abandoning the attempt to make it. The world of states has failed so far, but mankind is still young. We are familiar with the similar inspiration that found expression in the Nuremberg trials after the Second World War, with the difficulties, shortcomings, and criticisms that this more recent attempt has encountered.

[1] On the French attempt to detach the Saar from Germany and the compromise that was reached over that issue, see below.

In any case, Germany in 1919 was saddled with the costs of the damage of war, the full amount of which was to be set later on. That the amount was enormous was clear, and, apart from the moral aspect of the matter, some thought was given to the economic and financial possibilities, but rather little in 1919, when it was obviously easier and certainly more politically expedient to brandish the slogan "Germany will pay." In addition, as a preliminary to creating a world safe for democracy and peace, Germany, the aggressor, would be put on probation; she would be disarmed pending the day when, having worked her passage, she could be readmitted as a member in good standing of the community of states. Also, her preliminary disarmament could be interpreted as merely a first step on the road to universal disarmament.

In the subsequent knowledge of what has happened since, and granting that the misguided treatment of Germany was itself a contribution to the renewed breakdown of order, it may be difficult for us to understand how such things could be done. Yet the peacemakers of 1919 were neither inordinately wicked nor stupid. They were men motivated, as usual, by a variety of desires and interests. Most important, perhaps, one must remember that they had given voice to, and quite authentically reflected, some of the high hopes of mankind. The phrase "experiment noble in purpose" fits rather better the 1919 endeavors than those to which it was later applied.

There were other, and in the present context relatively minor, disabilities that were imposed on Germany. She was, for instance, deprived of all her colonies, a matter to which we shall return. Enough has been said, however, to make it clear that the terms of the peace were intensely resented in Germany, where they appeared as appalling and unjust and gave rise to a well-nigh unanimous surge of national opposition.

For nationalism was strong in Germany. The hopes of a better world, founded on justice, which had elicited response in that country as in others, had not simply and suddenly taken the place of deep-rooted tradition. The war, the immediate occasion of which had been a nationalistic issue, had itself done much to exacerbate national feelings. Hatred of Germany was deep in France, and for a brief moment it was no less intense in Britain, despite the supposedly greater stability and moderation of the British people.

The Settlement of Non-German Issues

The greatest success of the nationalistic force is to be found in Central and Eastern Europe. The Western states, as well as Germany and Italy, had become established on essentially clear national lines, and even the territorial losses of Germany left her main body in recognizable shape. There was no question in 1919 of dismembering Germany, despite some passing and feeble separatist velleities, for the simple reason that the people of Germany were German. Nor had there been, in the earlier part of the war, a clear determination to destroy the Dual Monarchy. Even the Italians had contemplated in 1915 no more than limited Adriatic gains, and the language of the Fourteen Points was cautious on the score of Danubian nationalities. Eventually, the Allies and America espoused unqualifiedly the cause of national independence in that region. This, to be sure, was useful to the purpose of war, but it could not have been done had not the fact and feelings of distinct nationalities existed. We have mentioned the disintegration of the Austro-Hungarian state in October 1918; it was an internal development.

This raised a host of problems for the peacemakers. To acknowledge that a Czech people exists is easy enough, but one must then proceed to answer the question, precisely where are the Czechs? This may not be so simple. The Wilsonian approach was best expressed in Point IX of the Fourteen Points, which referred to the Italian case and stated that "a readjustment of the frontiers of Italy should be effected along clearly recognizable lines of nationality." Wilson would ask his "experts" and then "fight for the right." The experts, American and others, produced a flood of memoranda on this question and on other similar ones.

In the West, say between Germany and France, the line of demarcation is sharp because of the long process of cultural crystallization. But the peoples of Central and Eastern Europe must go far back into their histories to find the existence of separate states, to a time when national feeling did not have the sharp clarity and consciousness that it acquired in the nineteenth century. Their political life, and to some extent their culture, had been submerged and overlaid by alien rule, Germanic in the main, and even some of their languages had only fairly recently acquired or reacquired literary stand-ing. The ruling class, the aristocracy, was often not overly imbued with national feeling, most consciously expressed and fostered by the literate bourgeoisie, the intellectuals above all. Moreover, the staunchest repository of the national lore was in many respects the peasantry, only partly literate, and sometimes more aware of reli-gious than of national distinction. Finally, there had been much intermingling of peoples.

The consequence of all this was that "clearly recognizable lines of nationality" were hard to determine, and it might also be men-tioned that, to a point, national and class conflict could merge or overlap: Polish landholders in Galicia dominated a Ruthenian peasantry, and Germans held a disproportionate place in the Bo-hemian world. Lastly, it should be pointed out that at the end of the First World War there was no suggestion of moving people about in order to make them fit frontiers. That neat and inhuman solution was reserved as a contribution of our more advanced time, but in 1919 it was thought that the land belonged to the people, to whom frontiers should in turn be adjusted.

Thus, in the Central European world, instead of sharp lines of demarcation one found broad zones of mixed populations, not to mention islands of one nationality scattered throughout and wholly surrounded by another. Yet frontiers must be lines in our modern conception; where to locate them was the problem. Some basic facts were used—censuses, for example, sometimes of dubious authenticity, and occasionally plebiscites. This last device, seemingly democratic and simple, in actuality is not such, for the outcome of it may depend on a prior decision as to the area in which the plebi-scite is to be held, and the voting may be influenced by many cir-cumstances, passing conditions, other than the presumably basic fact of nationality.

These were the fundamental conditions with which the peace-makers had to grapple in 1919, and to them might be added others, such as strategic, economic, and historic facts, the importance and validity of which could vary. It may come hard to Americans to acknowledge the legitimacy of long-passed situations, yet to general-ize on this score is impossible. Clearly, a claim based on the Roman conquest of Gaul or Britain would be a mere absurdity, but we know what has happened in the long Arab-inhabited Turkish province that was Palestine, as well as the fate of the Greek colonies of Asia Minor that had survived for two and a half millennia.

The appropriateness of the map of mid-Europe that emerged from the war has been questioned, not without cause, in some of its specific details. But with the best of will and the most impartial adjudication it could not have been otherwise than that many people should have found themselves on the wrong side of national frontiers: to avoid the existence of alien minorities, hence therefore of some discontent, was impossible. There were some especially sharp points of friction—Danzig between Germany and Poland, for example, and the whole Polish Corridor, Teschen between Poland and Czechoslovakia, Fiume between Yugoslavia and Italy, to mention some of the more widely advertised.

This last case serves as an illustration of another difficulty. The promises made by the Allies to Italy in the Treaty of London of 1915 were clearly not consistent with the American program for the peace, specifically with the ninth of Wilson's Fourteen Points. The Allies—Britain and France, that is—would not disown the validity of their signatures, but America was not bound by the Treaty of London. On the statistical facts of the situation there was little room for dispute. What to do? The quarrel was also between two states, Italy and the newborn Kingdom of the Serbs, Croats, and Slovenes, the existence of which had not been foreseen in 1915. The skill of the latter in placing their reliance on Wilson, on whose sympathy they could, as a small nation, count, stressed the Italo-American aspect of the issue. It was not necessarily beyond composition, but the combination of Wilsonian rigidity and righteousness with clumsy Italian manoeuvring resulted in an open clash and no solution at the time of the Paris gathering.

There was another significant aspect of this peculiar matter. At one point in the proceedings Wilson decided to issue a public statement of his position, an appeal to the world, including Italian opinion. He felt he was so right that if only his case could be heard none could fail to agree. Had he not, when earlier in Italy, received the authentically enthusiastic homage of the mass, to the extent that their own governors had been concerned with the display? It was for him a rude and sad awakening when this same Italian people responded with an outburst of overwrought, injured, nationalistic emotion, and the acclaiming cry of "Wilson!" was turned into *"vil sono!"* (I am vile). Here was perfect illustration with a vengeance of what could be done with the feeling of nationality.

Yet, allowing for imperfections and shortcomings, allowing also that such nationalistic emotions were understandably at high pitch immediately after the war, the fact remains that the postwar political map of Europe constituted the closest approximation in history so far to the ethnic map of that continent. This must be judged a very great accomplishment, provided, of course, that the validity of the principle of self-determination be granted. And, for all the aberrations of competing rival nationalisms, how deny the validity of the principle, founded as it is in the larger concepts of justice and of freedom? It might indeed be contended that, to take a random example, Poles would enjoy the advantages of better management at German hands than at their own. Such a contention is not necessarily invalid, but who would nowadays espouse it—who at least who has hopes of political office?—when even Black Africa is coming into its own? We have here a clear manifestation of the power of the deep forces of history.

But to return to mid-Europe in 1919, another sign of the prevailing spirit of the time may be seen in the fact that most of the states that were heirs of the Habsburg inheritance—Italy, a great power, was excepted—had to accept the obligation of minority treaties. This meant that the minorities within their borders were, theoretically at least, entitled to the protection of an external agency, the League of Nations. This obligation was resented, as well it might be, for it undoubtedly was an interference with the sovereignty of the state, an innovation that gave it all the more significance. How effective the attempt would be was another question, the answer to which time alone could provide. This was a measure of the impossibility of the task that was being attempted: there was high hope abroad that found expression in an effort to give birth to a New Order which the world was not yet ready to accept. In the perpetual clash between the past and the future, of which the present is made, *non fecit saltus natura* (there are no abrupt breaks in nature); yet unless the attempt is made change will never occur.

The overwhelming preoccupation of the peace conference with the German question was the inevitable consequence of the fact that Germany was the essential core of the enemy coalition as well as the director of its operation. But there was much more in Europe than Germany. The great problems of Europe after the First World War were in fact three. They bore the names of the three great defeated states, Germany, Austria-Hungary, and Russia, and of the three dynasties the war had destroyed, Hohenzollern, Habsburg, and Romanov. Unless and until these states or their heirs were brought back in some orderly fashion into the community of Europe, there could be no true peace on that continent.

The solution of the German problem having been elaborated in the Treaty of Versailles, the peace conference turned its attention to the Habsburg domain. The basic conditions that existed in that part of Europe have just been described, and by June, when the German treaty was signed, much preliminary work had already been done. The Habsburg monarchy was gone, and there was never any thought of attempting to put Humpty Dumpty together again. In dealing with the former Habsburg domain a fundamental distinction was made. The new states of Austria and Hungary proper were treated, like Germany herself, as enemy states, and the peace made with them was embodied in treaties patterned upon the Treaty of Versailles: the Treaty of St. Germain with Austria, signed in September 1919, and the Treaty of Trianon with Hungary, in June of the following year.[2] Like Germany, these countries were subjected to disarmament and to the obligation of paying reparations.

The rest of the Habsburg domain emerged from the war on the side of the victors. The new Czechoslovakia, wholly carved out of the former Austria-Hungary, was born of the desire for union of the kindred Czechs and Slovaks and had been recognized by the Allies before the war ended. The rest of the empire went to various surrounding claimants: Galicia became part of Poland; Rumania acquired Transylvania, the Bukovina, and part of the Banat; the Croats and the Slovenes joined their Serb brothers in the new triune kingdom of the South Slavs that eventually assumed the

---

[2] The Hungarian settlement suffered some delay owing to the temporary establishment of a Communist regime in that country during the spring of 1919.

official name of Yugoslavia. In this last respect the hopes of the Sarajevo assassins proved to have been justified. Some Croats and Slovenes came under Italian rule, for Italy obtained rather more than the *irredenta,* though not all that she had hoped from the Treaty of London. The Italo-Yugoslav situation, owing to the American veto, was not settled until November 1920, when a direct agreement was made between the two countries, which left in Italy a legacy of frustration and in Yugoslavia an understandable grievance and a suspicion of Italy's imperialistic designs.

Some Austrian Germans in the South Tyrol, about a quarter of a million, also came under Italian rule, for combined reasons of strategy, earlier treaty obligations, and apparently, Wilsonian oversight.[3] The greatest discontent, which to a point was justified, was felt by the Hungarians, minorities of whom where to be found in all of Hungary's neighbors, save Austria.

The thirteenth of Wilson's Fourteen Points had envisaged the resurrection of Poland, which was in addition to be given "secure access to the sea." The settlements devised in Paris established the frontiers of Poland in the north, the west, and the south[4] but of necessity left unsettled the eastern border, for Russia, or the Soviet Union, was not represented at Paris. Present or not, Russia could hardly be ignored, and there had been some attempt, which however did not succeed, to arrange for the sending of a Soviet delegation to the peace conference. The settlement with Germany, needless to say, not only wiped out the effects of that of Brest-Litovsk but created a vacuum for which a settlement would have to be devised.

The Russian situation differed from both the German and the Austro-Hungarian, dominated as it was by the fact of the Revolution. Russia in 1919 was involved in civil war, complicated by foreign interventions—American, British, French, and Japanese, not to speak of the presence of the Czech Legion in Siberia.[5] The Bolshe-

---

[3] It would appear that early in the proceedings Wilson had committed himself to the Treaty of London line as a frontier between Italy and Austria. Despite the opposition of his own experts, he did not feel that he could go back on his commitment.

[4] The settlement in Upper Silesia has been mentioned before. Poland also made good her seizure of Vilna, claimed by Lithuania.

[5] The Czech Legion, some 100,000 men, was made up in the main of deserters

viks for a time had sought to exploit the continuing war for their immediate advantage, maneuvering between both camps, but the defeat of Germany left them to face the Allies as the only effective power in being. The interventions of the latter, half-hearted as they were, helped confirm the Bolshevik leadership in their belief that the capitalistic world was bent upon their destruction.

The Bolsheviks commanded little real power, and though Trotsky performed a highly creditable job of military organization, their salvation was in the end the result of negative factors. The failure of coordination among counterrevolutionary forces was one; the other was the general weariness of war, as well as the response to the Revolution among their own peoples, which caused reluctance on the part of the Allies to use the force that they had, and which, if used with resolution, could probably have destroyed the revolutionary regime in Russia.

To the principle of self-determination the Bolsheviks subscribed. Control of the Baltic states and Poland had been wrested from them by the victorious Germans. Since the Allies in turn had endorsed self-determination and at the same time had no very tender feelings for either Bolsheviks or Germans, the result was the emergence of these states to independence. In their weakness, the Bolsheviks came to terms with and acknowledged these border states, Pilsudski's seemingly improbable judgment of 1915, that Poland's independence required a Russian defeat at German hands followed by a victory of the Western Allies, was precisely what had happened. But the Polish situation was not resolved until it had first come to open war with Bolshevik Russia. The war ranged far and wide, with alternating fortunes, from Kiev to Warsaw, until an equilibrium was reached and peace was made between Poland and Russia, establishing the eastern boundary of the former, in the Treaty of Riga in 1921. Thus, incidentally, Poland incorporated what was by far the largest minority in her state. With the settlement of her western frontiers[6] and the defeat of counterrevolution, revolutionary Russia was left to pursue her independent course.

---

from the Austro-Hungarian army. It did not adhere to the Revolution and was eventually evacuated by way of Siberia.

[6] All of Russia's western frontiers were settled, with the exception of the one with Rumania. The Soviet Union refused to recognize the *de facto* seizure of Bessarabia by Rumania, a fact recognized by the other powers.

Despite very substantial losses, both in territory and in population, Russia survived. But she was reduced to a state of incredible confusion and misery, even visited by famine. An enormous task of reconstruction was needed before the country could even return to the level of 1914, possibly to resume her development thereafter. Meantime, and for some time hence, Russia would count for little among powers; possessed of an ideological weapon alone, she would be left to her devices behind the *cordon sanitaire* designed to prevent the spread of her contagion.

Attention must be called to the unusual situation created by the fact that for an indefinite period two of the major states of Europe, Russia and Germany, would be reduced to a condition of impotence and hence could not make their voices felt in the councils of Europe. Of the three great problems of Europe that grew out of the war—Germany, Russia, and Danubia—none had been really solved by the peace. What is more, it is difficult to see what effective solutions could have been immediately devised. In this state of affairs lies much of the significance of the First World War.

2

Other Consequences of the War

Economic Consequences

Only the passage of time could assuage and soften exacerbated national feelings. Time likewise would be needed to make good the physical damage of war, which no arrangement of peace could of itself undo. Before 1914 there had existed a world-encompassing network of economic and financial relations. Stable currencies, trade balances, international exchanges of capital and goods had gradually developed in the midst of an expanding world economy, and they had largely come to be taken for granted. These exchanges, like individual travel, had been essentially free, unhampered by any appreciable degree of governmental interference.

To this state of affairs the war had brutally put an end, and mention has been made of the inevitable extension among all the principal belligerents of the functions and powers of the state. Just as war was considered unfortunate and its recurrence to be prevented, so there was after the war a widespread expectation that peace would bring a return to normality, meaning prewar conditions. Much of this hope was rooted in illusion, as the subsequent course of events would painfully establish, the same sort of illusion that tended to equate the cessation of fighting with the restoration of peace.

The single word that sums up best the economic effects of the war is *dislocation,* and there was no reason to assume that the scattered fragments would be put back together in their old pattern. Because of their own war demands, the European states had been unable to supply their foreign markets with the usual goods. Their place had been taken by others, most of all by the United States, to the expansion of whose industry and agriculture the war had given a great boost. The American manufacturer had no desire to relinquish a profitable market to its former suppliers merely because they had been such; why should he, under a regime of free competition? To a considerable extent the industrial plant of Europe was run down—some of it, as in France, wholly destroyed—and agricultural production was appreciably affected by the shortage of fertilizers.

There was everywhere a crying need for reconstruction, in the effecting of which the state had to assume a large role. The French case is a good illustration, especially because of the political and international complications that grew out of it. The view that the war had been a national undertaking was wholly fair, from which it followed that the consequent damage, be it human or material, was a proper charge on the nation. In France, as elsewhere, the state assumed the burden of war pensions. But the loser of property, the owner of a destroyed factory in the war zone, was likewise and with similar fairness compensated. The burden of these obligations mounted to astronomical proportions, certainly by comparison with what had been normal pre-1914 budgets.

This burden came on top of the financing of the war itself, and that too had far exceeded the expectations and what were thought to be the capabilities of pre-1914 economies. There was no outright bankruptcy in 1919, but all the belligerents emerged from the war with enormously inflated national debts, the British some tenfold, the German by a factor of forty. From the beginning, gold payments had been suspended and currencies had begun to fluctuate. While the war lasted there was cooperation among the Allies, and then with the United States, in controlling currency relations, but the pressure for a return to free economies caused the removal of controls and gave full scope to the manifestation of the effects of inflation.

The international aspect of finance was most troublesome. Foreign debts had been a normal component of the prewar international scene, one that was properly integrated into the network of international trade. The Central Powers had been largely cut off from foreign sources of capital, hence they had to rely on internal borrowing, but the American capital market was open to the Allies, of which they made full use. The difficulties they were about to encounter in continuing this practice were removed as a consequence of the American intervention. But in the First World War the view did not prevail, as it did in the Second, that the war was a common enterprise to which all should contribute according to their means. That brilliant invention, Lend Lease, was largely a product of the lessons of the First World War. In the earlier war America contributed unstintingly, but in the form of loans, to which further ones were added after the termination of hostilities for the purpose of reconstruction.[1]

The result, not the least important effect of the war, was to reverse the position of the United States from that of debtor to one of well-nigh universal creditor. The source of difficulty lay in the abruptness of the reversal, which had not grown out of a gradual readjustment of economic relationships but very suddenly out of the wealth-destroying fact of war. The significance of the transformation was little understood at first, not least in the United States where the need of understanding was greatest. Even after some years had passed an American President could sum up his view of the matter in the simplist comment, "Well, they hired the money!" This unexceptionable expression of New England moral rectitude in money matters was not so much wrong as it was irrelevant. For it was based on denial or ignorance of economic reality. The discharge of international financial obligations is inextricably tied to the balance of trade. Before the war it had been the proper thing for America to have a favorable balance of trade and be a debtor nation, just as the reverse was the proper condition for Britain. But the war reversed the debtor position of the United States while emphasizing more than ever her favorable balance of trade. It is not easy to see how America, by a deliberate act, could have in turn reversed the balance of trade, though she might have avoided aggravating the situation. The Fordney-McCumber Tariff Act of 1922 was not so much an expression of graspingness, let alone of moral wickedness, as of deficient economic thinking. But the problem remained, for which a near monopoly of the world's gold, stored under the ground,

---

[1] The large debts owed the United States became a very troublesome issue after the war. The discharge of these obligations, in economic terms, constituted a problem of precisely the same nature as that of the payment of German reparations.

could be no permanent solution. No other solution was found, unless one can call default and abandonment a solution, and the problem is still with us, though we now have at least some understanding of the issue and as a consequence no longer seek to deal with it in moral terms. But this is not the place to enter a discussion of the dreary record of international postwar financial relations; the intention is no more than to point out one aspect of the dislocation consequent on the war. Certainly the expectation that these things would take care of themselves once normality had been re-established was one of the more fanciful illusions of the immediate postwar period.

One more thing must be said of this subject, of which the French, or the Franco-German, situation is the best illustration. "Germany will pay" was a popular slogan in France, the expression of a pleasing prospect, reminiscent in its hopeful and naïve simplicity of President Coolidge's above-cited observation. The assumption in both cases was that the financial obligations that had grown out of the war would be added to previously existing ones and dealt with in the same fashion; had not the Ottoman and the Chinese empires, for example, discharged their debts? Why should not Germany?

There was, in the first place, the matter of the dimensions of the debt, plus the failure properly to take into account the connection between debt and balance of trade. In order to discharge an obligation of the size of that with which Germany was saddled, she would have had to establish so large a favorable balance of trade as to flood the world with her goods. Even if she had been capable of the necessary output, others, including France, would have sought to protect themselves from so threatening a competition by the erection of barriers. There are many ways of collecting reparations, but the attempt to do it in the form of external debt, payable within the framework of a free capitalist economy, respectful of free enterprise and of the rights of private property, as was done after the First World War, was indeed an impossible task. One may, if one wishes, see in it one of the so-called inner contradictions of capitalism.

Having suffered the greatest material damage, the French properly had the largest share in reparations, hence the greatest interest in securing their collection. The Franco-German relationship that for a time centered around this problem was highly disturbed, as well as disturbing to others, but we shall not at this point enter into the details of a tale at once fantastic and dreary. These things are now quite clear and the lesson well learned, but there were in the earlier stages very few warning voices of caution. Some there were nonetheless, arising, appropriately, in Britain, for in Britain, the great trading nation, one would naturally expect to find the best understanding of the problems of international trade and finance. John Maynard Keynes' since famous book, or diatribe, *The Economic Consequences of the Peace*, originally appeared in January 1920 and was an immediate sensation. The Keynesian influence has since become all-pervasive in economic theory and practice. Keynes' critique was a prescient one, though the acerbity of his pen, if it helped the success of his book, had also the effect of giving widespread vogue to other, less helpful myths where the general nature of the peace was concerned. The Four were *not* so many witches concocting an unholy brew in their cauldron.

Two years later, in 1922, the British government took the initiative of calling for an all-around cancellation of the debts growing out of the war, German reparations as well as Allied debts to America. It was an intelligent move, not a selfish one, save perhaps in the sense of enlightened self-interest, since on paper at least the British were on balance a creditor nation. The British proposal found no response. The American electorate was as uncomprehending of the necessity of canceling honestly contracted debts as was the French of the desirability of exonerating the Germans from the just retribution of their deeds. Economics was confused with ethics, and for a time the era of illusions continued to attempt the realization of the impossible.

The League of Nations

The related ideals of universal peace and of the unity of mankind have ancient roots. Western civilized mankind has known the unifying dominion of Rome and the benefits of the *Pax Romana*. When Rome fell upon evil days Christianity became the heir to the concept of universality, but the Church failed to secure either political unity or the universality of religious allegiance. The so-called modern period of history is introduced by, among other things, a further break in Christian unity, the Reformation, and the modern leadership of Europe has been characterized by the primacy of the sovereign state. Despite the setbacks, however, the appeal of the unitary ideal as well as of that of universal peace persisted. To say nothing of the empty shell that became the Holy Roman Empire, mention may be made of Henry IV of France's Grand Design, of some aspects of eighteenth-century thought, and of nineteenth-century Utopians. Tsar Alexander I's Holy Alliance, the Concert of Europe, the balance of power, all bear a certain relation to the desire to maintain at least a measure of order and peace in the otherwise anarchical community of sovereign states. Some manifestations might be cited, abortive as they remained in practice, of the continuing trend of thinking: writings of jurists, Hague conferences, interparliamentary union, the Swiss Committee for the Organization of Durable Peace, the English Union of Democratic Control.

There was also in 1914, from the mere fact of the duration of peace among the major European powers, a marked tendency to believe, or to hope, that the armed peace might prove lasting. The aftermath of Sarajevo destroyed all this while it showed the fragility of the balance of power. But the duration of the conflict, its obvious cost, and the havoc it wrought also had the contrary effect of strengthening the belief that the establishment of peace on a firm and durable basis was a greater imperative than ever. The League of Nations Society, founded in London in 1915, the French periodical *La paix par le droit,* the German *Friedensgesellschaft,* were expressions of this tendency, but it was logical that the stronger impulse should come from the neutrals removed from the immediate heat of the conflict. In January 1915, in the United States, was organized the League to Enforce Peace, which enlisted a number of notable personalities and conducted an active propaganda under the direction of former President Taft and with the sympathetic endorsement of the incumbent administration. Wilson himself endorsed the idea in speeches that he delivered in 1916 and 1917.

The idea was not primarily his own, but his final espousal of it, especially after the American intervention, clearly put it in an altogether different light, since it now had the support of the most powerful belligerent. This is what warrants the intimate association between the attempt to organize peace and the American President, warrants in fact his being credited with the fatherhood of it. The Fourteenth Point was Wilson's own especial contribution. Not only that, but by the time Wilson came to the peacemaking the concept of an "international association of nations" had become the chief center of his interest; the rest of the peace, frontiers and such matters, were relative details that could be settled on the advice of his experts. This approach, more than anything else, was the basis for Clemenceau's "noble candor" remark.

By the time the peace conference met, the idea that war was a nefarious activity, that the holocaust just ended must not be allowed to recur, commanded overwhelming assent in all quarters, not least among the former belligerents. The question was how to bring about this happy state of affairs. At the level of generalities there was still universal agreement: first, a peace of justice would eliminate future sources of conflict; secondly, the attempt must be institutionalized. On the score of the first, something has already been said of the divergent, not to say irreconcilable, interpretations of the content of "justice." Bright as the promise of the New Order might be, and much as all might want it, it is not possible at any point of time to make a *tabula rasa* of the past, least of all at the end of a war which has so inflamed national feelings. Even the well-meaning "experts" could not always agree, however much they might share honesty of intentions. As to the second, out of it was born the Covenant of the League of Nations, rather more aptly named in its French version, Society of Nations.

This document has been discussed elsewhere at great length and by many writers, and we shall be content in this treatment with some of its principal aspects. The ways of lawmaking are of necessity inimical to simplicity—some find them devious and tortuous—but in any event, one thing is clear from the beginning. The condition of order which has come to prevail within the modern state is based on the supremacy of law, the adjudication and interpretation of which is the task of the courts, and the enforcement of which rests in the last resort upon the entire power of the state. In the attempt to translate this condition of order under law to the international level, what shall be the equivalent of the court, and what shall be the law-enforcing agency in case of necessity? No one has yet contended that at the domestic level the acceptance of theory eliminates the need of coercive devices; put it another way, the citizen is not sovereign. In strict logic, therefore, sovereignty and international law are inconsistent notions. In this lies the key to many problems that have not yet been resolved.

This is the point at which a divergence appeared in 1919 in discussions of the League, a divergence that, broadly speaking, may be described as one between the English-speaking peoples and others—the latter, in 1919, because of their central position in the peacemaking, meaning largely the French. This may seem strange at first sight, yet really is not, for the difference may also be put in terms of that between the primacy of dependence upon sea power and land power respectively. Before 1914, before the air age, the element of time in military operations, barring surprise attack, favored the former. The difference therefore was essentially an honest one, born of differing circumstances and historical experiences. Here logic may be said to have been on the side of the French, that the establishment of any international order was inseparable from the making of concrete and dependable arrangements for its enforcement in case of need. This position, if logical, had the disadvantage of opening up an enormously complicated field of discussion, so intricate indeed that we are still struggling with its unresolved difficulties.

Wilson had at first approached the problem by placing emphasis on the necessity of disarmament and of a collective guarantee of the territorial integrity of the members of the international organization. He had subsequently been converted to the need of military sanctions, then reconverted back to his original view. Apart from possible constitutional difficulties that might be raised in his own country, there was the matter of the British view. The outcome, to make a long tale brief, was a discussion that was essentially Anglo-American, out of which came a draft that reconciled the differences between its participants. The French had virtually no share in this discussion, and their cherished scheme of an international force was lost in what became the final version of the Covenant of the League. This result, not surprisingly, had the effect of substantially diminishing what enthusiasm there had been for the League on their part. Their point, that it offered them little guarantee of security, was undoubtedly well taken.

Nevertheless, it is well to point out that politics is an exercise in the art of the possible rather than one in strict logic. The British and the American reluctance to assume commitments in peace time was a fact and a tradition that had served both countries well; hence their understandable tendency to insist upon the value of such factors as the moral power of opinion. Also, granted its imperfections and limitations, the League might be a useful beginning, with possibilities of growth, hence an experiment worth trying. If it was obviously too much to ask the French, and others, to trust their future safety to luck and possibly naïve hope, might not the Anglo-American guarantee provide adequate insurance pending the day when all would be equally safe under the effective guarantee of all? The institutions of mankind are not born full grown to perfection but forever evolve to meet new needs and circumstances. There is not a little merit in the Anglo-American gradualist and evolutionary approach which, it cannot be overemphasized, is in large measure the result of two things not enjoyed by others in the same degree: the well-rooted experience of smooth domestic development in governmental practice, and the equally firmly rooted feeling of security vis-à-vis the outside. It is tempting, in passing, to point out the perhaps distressing irony of the extent to which America has by now come around to the French position of 1919 and after. Like the French at that time, America no longer feels overwhelmingly secure in her own power and her geographical position. In any case, the Covenant of the future League of Nations, as drawn up in 1919, was essentially an Anglo-American document, in which fact lay a congenital limitation.

One more thing may be mentioned at this point, which is also, in retrospect, not devoid of irony. The Covenant of the League was incorporated as the introductory section of the Treaty of Versailles, although it had nothing to do with the German treaty as such. This was done in deference to Wilson's wish, and his point was indeed well taken: since peace with Germany was inescapable, so would be membership in the League, which might not necessarily have been the case had the Covenant been made a separate instrument. Something will be said presently of the unexpected consequences of this piece of logical reasoning. In addition, while the ultimate scope of the League was universal, Germany was excluded at first. As previously indicated, Germany in 1919 was on trial; once she had worked her passage and, hopefully, all had embarked on the road of disarmament, she might be allowed to join the circle of the virtuous. Needless to say, there was initially no question of League membership for the Soviet Union, currently dedicated to the destruction of the governmental institutions of the rest of the world. The Soviet Union, if successful in her hope of world revolution, would solve the problem of universal peace in a different way.

Despite all its congenital ambiguities and shortcomings, the League did embody a high ideal and great hopes. The slogan "the war to end all wars" enjoyed in many quarters even greater popularity than that "to make the world safe for democracy." Deep and sincere was the yearning of peoples for peace, and the significance should be neither minimized nor forgotten of the fact that this was the first time when a large group of states had formally underwritten an international constitution. It was at the very least a long step forward from the Holy Alliance or the Concert of Europe. The League also expressed in its structure the merger of the ideals of democracy and peace. It was patterned after the classical arrangements of parliamentary systems. In the Assembly the sovereign equality of states was sanctioned by the unitary vote, just as the classical principle of the democratic state gives every citizen an equal voice. The upper house, the Council, was the real repository of power; it was in recognition of the facts of power that the great powers were granted permanent representation in it, the rest to be elected by the Assembly. Also, the unanimity rule, which we now call the veto, prevailed in the Council.

The League was an untried instrument, and time alone could reveal whether another Utopia would be stillborn, to join the long roster of earlier dreams of perfection, or whether a new age in the relations among states had truly been inaugurated. Especially among the leaders of governments the attitude was one of considerable scepticism, ranging from the hopeful to the scornful, but the significance must be stressed again of the formal institutionalization of the attempt, as well as of the fact that from its very beginning the League was entrusted with a considerable range of specific responsibilities: the Saar, Danzig, the supervision of minorities treaties and mandates, to cite but some examples. The League was at the very least an expression of the widespread, if unfocused, acknowl-edgment that something must be done about the evils of the past, a broad yearning that did not exclude a simultaneous longing for a return to what seemed in contrast the good old days of a well-ordered past.

The Social Impact of the War

The intensity and the direction of the desire for the new shape of the future naturally depended upon the impact of the war on individuals and classes. War is a great promoter of change, not least at the social level.

Despite the steady spread of the democratic ideal, aristocracies had still had a large part in the direction of pre-1914 society. They had paid the blood tax and been thoroughly decimated in the war, but the war had been democratic in the sense that the blood tax had been exacted from others as well. On the revulsion against in-discriminate slaughter there was, in 1919, agreement, but the feel-ing was also abroad that the pre-1914 ruling class and élite had failed, which in a sense they indeed had. The sharpest manifesta-tion of this reaction was, of course, in Russia, where revolution was making a *tabula rasa* of the old order. But the most immediately significant aspect of the Russian upheaval was not so much the application of unsuitable Marxist theories, born of industry, as the reform of land tenure. The example was contagious and encouraged the native forces of change elsewhere. Throughout most of Central and Eastern Europe the old system of vast landholdings had seen its last days, and the small peasant landholder came into his own. Interestingly, this phenomenon fitted to a degree with nationalist movements. It was, from the standpoint of the new states, convenient that large estates in now Rumanian Transylvania, for example, should have been in Magyar hands, and a comparable position was that of the Germanic Baltic barons.

The peasants, for the rest, had rather profited in economic terms from the fact that they were responsible for so vital a sector of the war effort as the food supply. They had evinced their usual recal-citrance toward regulations; price controls, for example, were espe-cially difficult to enforce in their case. This situation was very noticeable in France. The industrial workers had fared not quite so well in this respect, though the needs of the war industries had given them, unlike the peasants, some benefit of military exemptions. But as prices rose, wages failed to keep up with them, a situation very marked in Britain. This condition tended to right itself in the later stages of the war and immediately after its termination, so that the working class was not, on balance, seriously injured; discontent in it was strong nevertheless. We shall not repeat here what has been said of the gradual revival of international socialism, Zimmerwaldian admonitions, and the Russian Revolution itself. This last event had very early, though divergent, effects on the working class movement. On the one hand, the Russian Revolution was a natural pole of attraction that suggested the possibility of reviving the prospects of the Second International. This in fact the Bolsheviks consciously and deliberately tried to do, both on account of ideological conviction and for the more limited and immediate purpose of saving the Revolution in Russia. The appeal met with encouraging response, and the figure of Lenin became a lode star rivaling that of Wilson. There was, during the very time when the peace was being drafted, much concern on the part of the other governments about the Bolshevik danger. We may refer again to the Hungarian and the Bavarian episodes,[2] and to the Allied interventions in Russia; when locked in difficulties with Wilson, the Italian representatives resorted to the argument, among others, of the Red Bogey if Italy did not receive satisfaction. Not a few thought the danger of revolution was real, until she found a self-appointed savior in the person of an ex-Marxist, Benito Mussolini.

But the Russian attempt to annex the leadership of the socialist movement, the Third International, turned out to be a failure. Inserting itself into the older quarrel between Mensheviks and Bolsheviks, and in the face of the latter's intransigence and insistence on discipline on the basis of an essentially Russian leadership, the Third International ended by causing a split in the socialist movement. The major part of the Western socialists continued to adhere to the evolutionary, gradualist view that had been theirs before 1914. From 1919 the terms *Communist* and *Socialist* have

[2] Just as in Hungary a Communist regime took control for a brief time in the spring of 1919, so in Bavaria there was also a short lived Communist episode.

stood for the distinct tendencies that are still familiar. Both claim descent from the same Marxist gospel and look to the same ultimate organization of society; being brothers, and perhaps just because they are brothers, differences and the intensity of vituperation, especially from the Communist quarter, have sometimes been more intense than those between either of them and the common capitalist enemy. To match the old phrase about the inner contradictions of capitalism, the inner inconsistencies of Marxism have now become equally familiar. Perhaps Marxists might profit from a study of Church history and of the enthusiasm with which Christian sects have disputed. But all this does not mean that the Russian example did not have a very great impact from its beginning, often especially among the rank and file of the working class, whose voice in any case would henceforth have to be more carefully heeded.

Inflations and fluctuating currencies were phenomena relatively unknown in the financially stable world of pre-1914. The enormous expenditures that the conflict entailed opened up unprecedented possibilities of gain. The war was the creator of fortunes, of a class of *nouveaux riches* whose profits were but little curtailed by taxation. Conversely, those who depended on fixed incomes—state employees, landlords, the classical small *rentier*—trustful of the dependable solidity of gilt-edged state securities, found their incomes and their positions correspondingly diminished. The really great inflations that totally destroyed the value of currencies occurred after the war, but the seeds of them were planted during the war years. Many of the victims did not understand the source and the nature of the difficulties that beset them. Their discontent, the search for scapegoats, was no less, and the war had the effect of producing a reshuffling of status, especially among the bourgeois middle class. The precise range of this social phenomenon is difficult to measure, but of its deep significance there can be no doubt. It is among this group of sufferers that was to be found the greatest hankering for a return to the good old days.

To sum up: unrest, dissatisfaction, yet great hope, were compounded in the climate of the immediate postwar period and made it a time of high instability. The future must be different, hence better, than the past; at the same time, the stability of the past must be recovered. And the peace was expected to realize all the contradictory hopes nourished by every individual and every segment of society.

3

The Reception of the Peace

The words that best sum up the reception of the peace are *disappointment* and *frustration*, which were not long in coming. The terms of the treaty of peace with Germany were received in that country with a reaction of stunned shock. How could this be the peace of justice promised by the New World Messiah with the assent of his associates? There was in Germany no special sense of guilt and little appreciation of the good fortune that had caused the fighting and the consequent damage to take place in other peoples' lands. Some loss of territory had of course been expected, but that substantial numbers of superior Germans should now be placed under the rule of inferior Poles was sheer outrage; the Polish border was henceforth the "bleeding frontier." Likewise, it had been expected that some payment would have to be made, but the dimensions of the German obligation, especially when introduced by the moral judgment of guilt, was injury compounded with insult. And the other provisions of the peace—Germany's unilateral disarmament, for example, or the deprivation of imperial possessions—were conclusive evidence of the punitive, revengeful intent of the peace that the thin veil of the professed high purpose of the peacemakers could not conceal. It was not peace but a *diktat*, that there was no choice in accepting, but which some time must be undone. This reaction was well-nigh unanimous. This is not the place to assess the merits or shortcomings of the German treaty, the validity of the German grievance, the wishful thinking and unwarranted illusions, or the legends that were cultivated in Germany; the point to be emphasized is the fact of the German reaction. The only observation to be made on this score is that the German disappointment was perhaps in large measure inevitable, though doubtless the particular form of some of the terms of the treaty was well designed to rub unnecessary salt into inescapable wounds.

Speaking of bleeding frontiers, the case of Hungary had far better foundation than the German, and if the world has been less familiar with it that is only because Hungary is a small power. The Austrians had less cause for discontent on this score; many of them were ready to forget the past glories of the House of Habsburg and to become a province of the German Reich. This the peace forbade them to do save with the unlikely consent of the victors. The arguments for and against the *Anschluss* will not be considered here. It was understandable that the desire for it should exist, but it was also reasonable that after a war which had taken the efforts of a world coalition to defeat Germany the feeling should prevail that German power should not be enhanced by the accretion of a substantial piece of territory and some six and a half million people. Where the enemy was concerned, much that was written in the settlements of peace had been implicit in the war itself.

The Habsburg monarchy was dead, and though some regretted its passing, there was little talk of its resuscitation. But the problem of Danubia remained, and the dangers inherent in the further Balkanization of Europe were obvious. What to do? The force of nationalism could not be denied, and the new nationalisms, whether victors or vanquished, not surprisingly tended to be vigorous, overwrought, and suspicious. Most of them had substantial minorities within their borders, and they all needed for their future economic viability the cooperative sort of approach that the tariff-making prerogative of newly acquired sovereignty was the least calculated to produce.

But to the victors also the fruits of victory were hardly sweet. France was but one among the Allies, hardly the most powerful, but her special place and her contribution to the war gave her a central and a highly important voice in the shaping of the settlements. That Germany should be laid low might be contemplated with satisfaction, but France had been truly bled white. Her irreplaceable dead she could only mourn; the wreckage of her factories and fields Germany could eventually make good, though reconstruction could not wait for long-deferred compensation. France was in 1919 *the* great land power of Europe, but in that momentary magnification of her power she found little cause for elation. Realistic Clemenceau had sought to capitalize on the advantage of the circumstances and thought that if he could insure the safety of his country for a generation he would have deserved well of her. For the long term—and quite rightly as it turned out—the French felt deeply concerned for their security and fearful of the limitations of their own power. When the Treaty of Versailles was submitted for ratification to the French Parliament, the government presented it in apologetic fashion: imperfect as it was, it was the best that could be had, for the wishes of France's allies, America and Britain in particular, had had to be taken into consideration and deferred to. France came out of the war, strange as it seemed to many at the time, with a feeling of insecurity, also with a sensation of intense lassitude.

There was fatigue and weariness in Britain too, but the British reaction was less clear than the French. From one standpoint, the war inserted itself easily into the British tradition: as on earlier occasions, Britain had successfully fought for the preservation of the European balance of power, and the Kaiser had gone the way of Napoleon. Also, as usual, Britain had enhanced her imperial position. Britain nevertheless was aware that the cost had been high, not only or so much perhaps through actual expenditures as in terms of lost commercial place. Sunken ships and lost markets are less easily perceivable than destroyed factories; they are not a less serious loss for that, and markets in particular are harder to replace. Britain was acutely aware of the rise of the American giant, whose naval power could easily outmatch her own and whose economic stature was overwhelming. The problem of recovery and of adjustment to diminished position was not a simple one and was not to be faced with unrestrained confidence.

Italy's participation in the war had in a way been a miscalculation. She had, to be sure, correctly picked the winning side, but the war had been long and harsh and had placed a severe strain on the weaknesses of her economy, no less than on her still-developing institutions. To cap it all, the peace had gone wrong and Italy had not obtained even the contractual price of her intervention. Instead of satisfaction on the completion of the work of the Risorgimento and on the opportunities that the demise of Austria-Hungary might offer in mid-Europe, there was much talk in Italy of "mutilated victory" and of "lost peace." There was also much social unrest, and the outcome of the war and the peace gave renewed comfort to those who had initially opposed participation in the conflict. The very victory to which she herself had contributed had also robbed Italy of the most valuable asset of her foreign policy, the equilibrium of power, for the thoroughgoing impotence of Germany placed France, for the moment at least, in a dominant position.

But in some ways the most interesting case of all was that of the United States. Compared with those of the other belligerents, American casualties were insignificant. America had lavishly contributed material resources and financial assistance, but the war had vastly benefited her economy, belying the uncritical judgment that from modern war no one ever profits. The power of the United States at the end of the war in all respects far outdistanced all others, a fact so obvious that it was universally acknowledged. Correspondingly, the American influence in the shaping of the peace had been very large.

Because of the experiences of the last fifty years it has become rather unfashionable to speak of idealism, especially in the domain of the relations among states, where the harsh facts of power rule. It is indeed difficult for the present battered generation to recapture the atmosphere of fifty years ago, attempts to describe which are likely to elicit a reaction of cynical doubt and a suspicion of fraudulence; we often think that we are no longer naïve. That foreign affairs had had a relatively small impact on the American people is as true as the fact that Americans are in the last analysis not insensitive to their own interest. But it is also true that the position of America in 1919 was different from others. The relatively puny squabbles which had been the stuff of the relations among European powers were alien to America, and if there is some warrant for the charge of naïveté directed to the Wilsonian approach—"Tell me what's right, and I'll fight for it!"—the approach nevertheless expressed a high standard. Through Wilson, the overwhelming weight of American influence was devoted to the effort to draw the world out of the traditional morass of power competition into the higher realm of law. And thus the League was born.

But here a curious thing happened, for as it turned out in the
reckoning, America proved to be the most jealous guardian of sovereignty. The constitutional arrangements of the United States provide for the ratification of treaties by a two-thirds majority of the
Senate. The events of the summer and autumn of 1919, the argument that centered around the possible limitations of American
sovereignty consequent upon membership in the world organization, the errors of commission and omission in the handling of the
situation, the accidents of personality— the intransigent rigidity of
Wilson, the smallness of the gentleman from Massachusetts, Henry
Cabot Lodge, Republican Chairman of the Senate Foreign Relations Committee—are all familiar things. The outcome alone matters at this point, the failure of the United States to ratify the Treaty
of Versailles.[1] It was an awkward situation when the child whose
acceptance had been forced upon others was then disowned by its
own father. The consequences of this unforeseen state of affairs belong to a later story; that they would be considerable is the least
that could be expected.

To this failure to ratify the German treaty of peace there was a
footnote, perhaps fraught with even greater consequences for the
immediate future. We must recall the compromise out of which the
French desire for security had been assuaged by the promise of an
Anglo-American guarantee. The treaty which embodied this arrangement never even reached the floor of the Senate for discussion,
dying instead in pigeonhole. That French security should be a remote problem to the Senator from Idaho or California, worthy of
little concern, is easily understandable; it is equally understandable
that the French should feel otherwise. More serious was the fact
that in the *quid pro quo,* the bargain that had been evolved in the
spring of 1919, one side, the French, had delivered its price—it was
written into the German treaty—while the other, America, declined
to do so. The contemplation at this point of American constitutional practice could obviously afford but little comfort. The American action constituted an invitation to the French to seek alterna-

---

[1] Technically, this left the United States in a state of war with Germany. The
subsequent Treaty of Berlin in 1921 restored formal peace between the two
countries. It is of interest that that treaty was essentially identical with the Treaty
of Versailles, minus the Covenant.

tive solutions. This they did, though ultimately not with the best of results. Perhaps the most regrettable aspect of it all was that an American guarantee, for a very small price and risk, offered the possibility of being the most effective deterrent of German aggression, should such be contemplated in future, while correspondingly, by giving adequate satisfaction to the French desire for security, it could have facilitated the adoption by France of a different policy, not to mention the fact that it would have given America a measure of control over what later came to be regarded as the less desirable aspects of French policy.

We must return to the League for a moment. The League was an experiment, untried, of the prospects of which it was equally legitimate to hold a sceptical or an optimistic view. Like all institutions or treaties, the League was perhaps not so much good or bad in itself. It reflected conditions and views at a specific point of time, and the main issue was the use that would be made of the instrument. The possibilities were diverse. It could serve in disguise as a device for confirming and freezing the iniquities of the *status quo* —assuming that it was iniquitous—as some feared and others hoped that it would do, but the League could also be used as an instrument for the smooth accomplishment of change. The League was also charged, or burdened, with a number of specific responsibilities.

The German Saar was not annexed by France; it was, under League supervision, temporarily detached from Germany for fifteen years, after which time its fate would be settled by plebiscite. The creation of the Free Territory of Danzig has been mentioned. It is an interesting reflection that the Saar rejoined Germany in 1935, after the plebiscite was held, while in Danzig was found the occasion for the outbreak of the Second World War. The League was also made the keeper of the minorities treaties and of that other innovation, the mandates. About the last something more must be said.

When the British were confirmed in the possession of Cape Colony and Malta at the close of the Napoleonic Wars, the right of conquest was the clear and simple basis of their title. After the First World War Germany was deprived of all her overseas possessions; had things remained as they were until the American intervention, the German colonies would have been shared in accordance with the prearranged plans of the Allies. The plans for the disposition of the Ottoman Empire have also been indicated. All this was in keeping with traditional practice.

America sought for herself no territorial acquisitions, imperial or other. In addition, reflecting her own origins, America was prejudiced in favor of the independence of any people who asserted the desire for that condition. Before 1914 the empires of the various European states seemed securely established and were in fact still expanding, if for no other reason because of the respect that European power commanded. European conquest had the inevitable effect of introducing to the conquered colonies European ideas, among which nationalism and the Rights of Man loom large. But the progress of such ideas was still very small among dependent peoples, though one may mention Indian stirrings and the beginnings of similar developments in the Arab world. The spectacle of the powers of Europe locked in deadly struggle and the enlistment by Europeans of colonial contingents for the purpose of fighting other Europeans had not failed to register on the dependent peoples. It did little to enhance European prestige among them, and at the same time it made large numbers of them familiar with the ways of Europeans at home. There was in 1919 little apparent threat of colonial revolt, the seeds of which would take further time to mature. But the high purpose of the war, of which America was the best spokesman, fitted ill with the traditional bartering of peoples.

President Wilson had faced the issue, and in the Fourteen Points expressed what can only be called an eminently sane view. While the validity of the right to independence was acknowledged, there was also recognition of the fact that many peoples were not ready for self-government. Consequently, the claims and the positions of the imperial powers should be given due weight as well as the care and the rights of their dependents. It is from this approach that the concept of mandates was born, an American as much as a British contribution. Title to the former German possessions and to parts of the Arab section of the Ottoman Empire would be turned over to the League, and the League would in turn appoint "mandatories" whose task it would be to "guide" the mandated territories toward eventual independence. In further recognition of difference in stages of political development, mandates were classified into three categories, A, B, and C, from the most to the least advanced.

As it turned out, the attribution of mandates followed the lines of the arrangements previously made among the Allies. Was this a clever sleight of hand, the climax of hypocrisy and cant for which the League offered a most convenient cloak, a skillful refurbishing of the older white man's burden or *mission civilisatrice* argument? The suspicion existed and the charge was made. Or was it truly an innovation in the imperial domain, a concession to an inescapable force to be put in the same category as that which had led to the universal franchise? There were also those who genuinely accepted the latter interpretation. Who really could in 1919 answer with assurance a question to which the passage of time alone could furnish a reply?

But at the very least it must be granted that the League was a bold innovation, more than any other single aspect of the First World War settlement the expression of the hopes to which the war itself had given rise. The League, we know, failed, though it is highly significant that after another world war we have been able to think of nothing better than a slight variation of it, the present United Nations, the fate of which still hangs in uncertain balance. Our current expectations are more modest, and we think that we now have a more realistic appreciation of the facts of power, as well as of the forces that move societies and individuals. Perhaps we are merely indulging in another form of naïveté. However that may be, the verdict may be granted that the discrepancy and the clash between the too high expectations to which the war itself had given rise and the reality of a multitude of concrete situations and stresses made the task of 1919 an impossible one.

III

The Meaning

1

The Aftermath

So far this essay has endeavored to sketch, first, the background of the situation that resulted in the outbreak of war in Europe in 1914, then the effects of the war on the European complex and its operation, with some attention as well to the consequences of the American participation. If the initial view, that unless Germany secured an expeditious victory the greater resources of the Allied camp would favor its success, had in the outcome proved correct, that result came about in unexpected fashion. Russia fell by the wayside in the process, and her place was taken by the United States, the final architect of victory.

These unforeseen developments, and the duration of the war, with its unimagined demands on the peoples, turned the conflict into something very different from what had been initially envisaged or from what may be called a classical war, that effects certain readjustments of power and position but leaves essentially unaltered the basic structure of the international community or the internal structure of its members.

Thus the war gave rise to contradictory expectations. The desire to be done with the unpleasant task of fighting, and the corresponding one to return to the familiar ways of interrupted occupations, commanded universal acceptance. This last wish may be equated with the conservative desire to return to the past; many looked back with nostalgia to the good days of 1914 and before. But there were in 1914 many currents that were making for change in a society which to many people seemed highly imperfect. After an initial period of quiescence, the war itself gave a new fillip to these forces, and the Russian Revolution, born of the war, was the sharpest manifestation of the influence of war as a promoter of change.

135

From a different quarter, the American, there came a similar promise of better things, of a New Order. The impact of the promise was considerable, and the American role in shaping the peace settlements has been indicated. But the peace by itself, whatever its shape and its quality, could only go a certain distance toward solving the deep-rooted tensions that, in varying degrees, stirred the hopes of men everywhere. In this concluding section, stress will be placed on the extent and shape of the break that had taken place.

The United States After the War

Here a distinction must be made. For although the usual description of the 1914 conflict as the First World War is warranted because of the effect it had on the whole world, the war was essentially a European affair. Among non-European states America alone was a truly significant participant, and even in her case the immediate impact of the war was very different from its impact on the European belligerents. To begin with, the active participation of the United States in the war lasted less than two years. The United States did not mobilize its manpower on a scale comparable to others; the discrepancy appears even greater if war losses are considered. There is no need of great imagination to appreciate that the American reaction to the experience of war would have been quite different had some 5 million American men been killed—a proportionate figure to the French or the German on the comparative basis of populations. The American people did not emerge from the war with an overwhelming sensation of weariness, nor was their confidence impaired by having seen the face of defeat at close range. It is therefore understandable that the United States should come out of the war with a feeling of optimistic confidence in itself, its power, and its future, and that it should approach in the same fashion the complicated task of reshaping the world into a new and better order.

This type of outlook fitted well into the whole background of the American experience. In comparative terms, the weight of the past did not lie heavy on the American nation, whose story is in large measure a tale of rapid and little-impeded growth and expansion. The phrase "America is promises" is apt.

This does not mean that in the final reckoning the impact of the war was less on America than on others. In simplest form, that impact may be summed up by saying that the war marked the coming of age of America in the community of states. The war did not create American power, the fundamental bases of which had existed for some time, but it brought the extent and reality of that power into the full light of day. The situation was in fact unique, if not destined to be of extended duration, which set American power in a position so far above any other. But the actual change of recognized position was too abrupt, and it is not surprising that the implications failed to register properly on the American consciousness, even in places where greater perceptivity might perhaps have been expected. The circumstances of geography and of history had together conspired to keep the American potential fairly well out of the main stream of world affairs, certainly by comparison with the intense activity of the great powers of Europe. Isolation was for America less a theory than an existing condition.

The consequences of this state of affairs were strange and hardly of the best, either for America or for others. Now that the task of war was done, successfully registered in victory, the pressure was very great to "bring the boys back home." Home they came, and the great American war machine was dismantled with distressing alacrity. Save on the Rhine, where Americans remained for a time, the task of policing where necessary was left to others, mainly the British and the French, especially the latter. The peace was something else; it should be prompt and good, under the aegis of democratic institutions, open covenants, and a world organization.

For this last there was much authentic support in America, but we shall not review the combination of circumstances that led to the rejection of the Treaty of Versailles. Once that had happened the recoil was swift. Wilson, though ill, stubbornly clung to office for the remaining year of his tenure, still fighting for the right as he saw it and for the things that he believed in. But, like himself, American influence was largely paralyzed. The election of 1920 may be seen as the turning point. For although the successful Republican party still paid unconvincing lip service to the League in the electoral campaign, the new administration soon set the course on isolation.

This is now often condemned, and though the condemnation is warranted, it is well to realize that the new orientation was fair illustration of the proper operation of the democratic process, since it authentically reflected the dominant wish of the American people. The disillusion with the peace had not been long in coming, and it came to be the fashion to blame the settlement for the ills of a world that was slow in recovering. From this it was but a short step to the view that America's participation in the war had been a mistake, hence that special care should be taken to avoid the recurrence of a similar situation.

This was the heyday of wishful thinking and illusion, born of dislike of facing awkward facts. The American people were ill served by their leaders, who, instead of seeking to educate them to the novel realities of a changed world, fostered and catered to their predilections. In Keynes' favorite words, which he applied to Wilson, the American people had been "bamboozled," and a long roster of scapegoats was discovered to share the guilt of having taken advantage of well-intentioned and idealistic American innocence. There were the native dark forces, epitomized in such figures as J. P. Morgan and his foreign loans, the "merchants of death" callously making gain from cannon fodder (profits from high-priced wheat or good employment in industry were on the whole conveniently forgotten), or alternatively the lies of foreign propaganda; all had combined to take advantage of American trust. Stories of German atrocities, some true, many invented, came to be widely disbelieved, and even scholars came into the fray. The revisionist school of historians prospered and in turn "bamboozled" a whole generation of well-intentioned future scholars.[1]

The most regrettable part of it all is that this strong response was born in part of the revulsion against war but also of the same well-intentioned desire for justice and for a better world which had led to the presumably erroneous act of entering the war in the first place. When the world horizon began clouding again, the American response was a pathetic attempt to legislate America away from

[1] The controversy that grew out of the war guilt clause of the German treaty resulted in much serious historical work. But the extent to which the moralistic approach entered the work, especially of American and British scholars, is a remarkable phenomenon in itself. Subsequent events have had the converse influence of inducing a revision of the revisionist thesis.

the rest of the planet. That was the gist of the Neutrality Acts: lest we be taken in again, we would eschew distinctions between right and wrong, treat alike the Abyssinian victim and the Italian aggressor, and smile in incredulous detachment at the reports of Nazi concentration camps. The debate on whether or not America was part of this world was still going on when the Japanese bombs resolved it at Pearl Harbor.

The point must be emphasized that the well-meant but uncritical reaction to the war of 1914 was one of wholesale rejection. Since the physical impact of that war had been relatively small, it was correspondingly easy to return to "normalcy," according to the slogan of the immediate postwar period. Shedding wartime controls and returning to the traditional ways of free enterprise, America prospered, cultivating economic no less than other illusions. The very prosperity, the accumulation of capital, caused dollars to flow like a golden shower to many parts of the world. This for a time made possible the absurd vicious circle of the payment of German reparations and of the Allied debts to America. The decade following the war seemed like a golden economic age, made slightly lurid by the experiment of prohibition, apart from which America could proceed to tend her garden untroubled by what went on in the rest of the world.

The reckoning did come, which may be seen as a manifestation of the unresolved dislocations that grew out of the war itself; such at least is a tenable view of the Great Depression of the 1930s. For America the economic crisis had far greater impact than the war had had, for the depression had the effect of deeply stirring all layers of American society as well as of introducing a new age of reform, of which the welfare state is the now generally accepted child. Leading into the Second World War as it did, these two experiences marked a real imprint on the American consciousness. The second war had the combined effect of confirming and accentuating the trend of social and economic reform, while simultaneously destroying the isolationist myth. It has taken thirty years and two wars to integrate America into the world community of states, and the effect of this passage has been the tendency in America to equate the Second World War with a major break with the past. This contention is valid at least as far as feeling and climate of opinion are concerned, despite the fact that in effect the real break occurred in the earlier conflict. The revolutionary effects of the First World War were perceived with far greater clarity in the active theatre of the war: in Europe.

The European Aftermath

To be sure, the feeling also existed among the European belligerents that a return to normality meant a return to the prewar situation. But Europe had been shaken by the war in a manner that America had not; from the European standpoint the Second World War is not so much the real and great break with the past as it is a completion of unfinished business that the first war left in its train. However strong the wish to return to the past—a wish, for that matter, that many did not share—clearly too much had happened that, in contrast with the American experience, it was impossible to ignore or deny.

Though for some time we have been hearing much on the subject of the current revival of Europe—a reality, yet a still-uncertain accomplishment—stress should rather be put on Europe's loss of place in the world, her demotion. Again, to American eyes the turning point seems to be the Second World War, when the collapse of France in 1940 may be cited as the single event that most sharply startled the American consciousness. By the time Germany had been destroyed, even physically in considerable measure, and it had become clear that Britain was limping instead of having recovered her position, it is not very surprising that the feeling should have been widespread that there was little left in Europe.

This picture has validity for the period that immediately followed the Second World War, but the real turning point for Europe had actually occurred a quarter of a century before. The half-century encompassed by the Franco-Prussian War and the First World War has been characterized as the Apogee of Europe. By 1914, with the qualifications of America and Japan, Europe was truly mistress of the planet and the center that furnished the motive power of its functioning, be it in terms of crude power and political control or in terms of commerce, institutions, and ideas. The effect of the war on this situation will most conveniently be examined under two heads: first, Europe in Europe, then Europe in the wider world.

Europe was a collection of long-established entities and contained five of the world's great powers. Whatever unity there was in Europe in 1914 lay in the heritage of common culture. Real and important as this was, in the domain of power the stress was on rivalry and competition rather than unity. If there was general agreement among Europeans in the consciousness of their superiority and in the consequent legitimacy of ruling most of the rest of the world, Europe maintained at home an uneasy peace resting on a delicate balance of power. What happened in 1914 was a break in the equilibrium, but this had happened before, and it has been explained that for some time the feeling continued to prevail that the war would effect some inner readjustments but would not otherwise materially change the fundamentals of the European system in Europe, or the position of Europe in the world as a whole. The war had precisely the effect of altering radically both conditions.

So long as kings were divinely appointed rulers, defeat in war did not necessarily impair the constitutional standing of a monarchical regime. But in the twentieth century even a Russian tsar could not withstand the disgruntlement of his subjects. Four ancient dynasties were destroyed by the war: the Romanovs, the Habsburgs, the Hohenzollerns, and the Osmanlis. But startling and significant as this may have been in itself, it was less so than the destruction of a state. The Ottoman may be regarded as a somewhat special case, owing to the role of Europe's imperial urge in it, but there had been no thought at first that Austria-Hungary, one of the components of the community of major powers, would simply be no longer. The unprecedentedly radical application of the democratic principle of self-determination had produced that outcome. Danubia was a problem indeed after its fragmentation, but there was little power in the separate fragments of Danubia.

This same principle of self-determination was responsible for an extensive Russian retreat and for some appreciable German losses. Unlike the Dual Monarchy, however, Russia and Germany remained as large and recognizable entities. But for the moment, and

for some indefinite future, there would be no power in either of
these states. Power was all in the hands of the victors, which, among
major powers, meant Britain, France, and Italy. This imbalance
alone was serious enough, but even the victorious coalition was
riven by inner stresses and dissents. For Italy, the strain of the war
combined with the destruction of the former European balance had
the effect of making that country count for even less in European
affairs than her intrinsic strength may have warranted. Disgruntled
and restless, like America seeking domestic and foreign scapegoats,
Italy adopted a policy of retreat and retrenchment and played a
role of self-effacement.

This left Britain and France. It is conceivable that an Anglo-
Franco-American combination, endowed with the power and the
stabilizing influence of America, might have led Europe back to a
situation where the defeated, Germany and Russia, could have been
reintegrated into the larger community, and thus at least have
avoided some of the stresses that their exclusion created. It certainly would be more difficult, though perhaps not wholly impossible, for Britain and France, together but without America, to lead
Europe back to some orderly functioning. For Britain and France
to fall out would, under the circumstances, be to court suicide. Yet
that is precisely what they did.

It is perhaps best to eschew moral judgment and an attempt to
apportion blame for such a state of affairs, but some examination
of the subject is necessary since it has much to do with the "political
collapse of Europe" [2] after, and as a consequence of, the First World
War. The roots of that outcome lie in the contrasting reactions of
the two countries to the war.

From the British standpoint, the war, as previously pointed out,
inserted itself easily in a familiar record, the successful prevention
of the establishment of *any* hegemony on the Continent. The British, as the phrase goes, have no permanent allies; they only have
permanent interests. An accurate enough characterization, that is
descriptive of the peculiar position of the world empire centered
on island Britain rather than of any special attribute of duplicity
in the British character. This view of things, however, by placing

---

[2] Hajo Holborn, *The Political Collapse of Europe* (New York: 1951).

stress on the factor of balance, had the understandable effect of making Britain sympathetic to some restoration of German power —for the sake of equilibrium. Perhaps the impact of the threat contained in Germany's overly rapid growth had been too brief to strike sufficiently deep roots, in contrast with the longer record of Anglo-German cooperation and Anglo-French rivalry. In this context the sentimental vagaries of feeling that soon turned much British opinion to a sympathetic view of maligned and mistreated Germany were but a minor added irritant in postwar Anglo-French relations. What matters is that the wartime Anglo-French duet soon turned into a postwar Anglo-French duel.

For the French view of things was very different. One could have drawn a glowing picture of French prospects immediately after the war. Germany lay prostrate, and in the Treaty of Versailles lay the means of prolonging her impotence. France was the one effective force in being on the Continent, once most of the Americans had gone home and the British had showed a strong inclination to reduce as much as possible their Continental commitments. The watch over Germany, the containment of Russia by the *cordon sanitaire,* the implementation of various clauses of the peace in various parts of Europe—plebiscites, for example—found the French at the forefront and French troops usually in the locality. France was the guardian of the order of Europe.

This was not the result of a French plan so much as the outcome of circumstance, and in a larger sense it may be said that for the France of 1920 to be the guardian and upholder of the European order was a too onerous, in fact an impossible task. For the position of France was wholly false and unreal because it did not correspond to the long-term facts of power. But what to do? Some form of international order had to be preserved in Europe. The one hope was that with the passage of time things would gradually change and others besides France, including above all defeated Germany and problematic Russia, would come to play their proper share.

The transition would have been difficult at best. Had France after the First World War been the France of Napoleon, she might either have maintained control by the use of adequately superior force, or conceivably, because secure in her own power, she could have allowed such a transformation to occur. But, strange as it seemed to many at the time, France, seemingly all powerful but badly injured and bled white by the war, was obsessed by the problem of her future security. The answer was therefore a staunch and narrow adherence to the letter of the law and an effort to pile guarantees upon reinsurance. It was a policy that led to intransigence and to the doing of some unpleasant things; it was also a policy that made the French highly unpopular in many quarters, not least among some of their former allies, as the chief obstacle to the restoration of peace, which in a sense they were.

Yet these former allies, the Americans and the British in particular, were the very ones who compounded the difficulty. America had rejected the Treaty of Versailles, hence the League, and declined to implement the guarantee to France. It was wholly natural in the circumstances that France should look for substitutes for this default. These were easily forthcoming. For there were a number of states in Europe which shared with France the wish to preserve the advantages they had derived from the war. Thus came into existence the French system of alliances, beginning in 1920 with Belgium, followed by Poland the next year, then Czechoslovakia, Rumania, and Yugoslavia. In addition, the last three of these states, on the basis of their common interest in Central Europe, more narrowly their opposition to Hungarian revisionism, joined in the separate combination known as the Little Entente. Where Hungary was concerned France had no very strong feelings, but she was quite willing, with an eye on possible precedent, to help maintain the *status quo* everywhere. France's concern was overwhelmingly with Germany, in which regard the prospect of Polish and Czech assistance loomed large in her eyes. Poland and Rumania also filled the role of advanced posts in the *cordon sanitaire*.

When the United States went back on the commitment of reinsurance to France, the British, taking advantage of an escape clause in the arrangement, followed suit, perhaps unwisely, thus emphasizing the isolation of the French position. Anglo-French difference was not long in finding cause for expression. When, at the end of 1922, the French decided to enforce the strict letter of the law in the matter of German reparations, they did this with Belgian support and with reluctant Italian acquiescence, but in the face of British condemnation. The episode of the Ruhr is an instructive passage. In the Franco-German test of strength that resulted Germany once more had to acknowledge defeat when Stresemann recognized the failure of the policy of passive resistance, which he consequently abandoned. The Ruhr may be said to have marked the high point of French unpopularity abroad, coincident with the assertion of French power. It was a misleading picture that resulted in an empty victory, for French power had successfully asserted itself when no effective challenge could confront it. The manner in which the French, about the same time, seemed to favor their Polish ally in the latter's seizure of Vilna and in the plebiscite in Upper Silesia, for example, served to confirm the picture of the abuse of French power and fostered the dislike, even the fear, of it by some. There was some point to Briand's irritated observation to the British that there would be more effective substance and weight to their criticism of the action of the French forces in Silesia if they themselves had been willing to furnish a larger contingent in that area.

Comparisons have been made between the earlier Bismarckian system and the postwar French security system. Both had one thing in common: their purpose was the preservation of the existing European order in peace on the basis of the *status quo* by the enlistment of overwhelming forces. In a sense it had required greater skill in the case of Bismarck, for although Germany and German power were the core of his system, he had had to deal with a number of equals over whom his influence was limited. In the case of the French system, by contrast, the French core was definitely the dominant element, to whom the rest stood in a relation of satellitic dependence. But precisely in this lay the flaw of the later combination. On paper the sum total of the armies and guns that the system could enlist was impressive indeed, possibly quite adequate to maintain the European order in existence, a fact contemplated with satisfaction in France. But this placed a correspondingly heavy responsibility on the French core of the alliances, for should that core show lack of resolution the whole edifice could easily collapse.

This is in fact what happened. For the French people were weary and lacking in the aggressive resoluteness that would have been needed to control Europe. We come here to one of the central facts of power: power does indeed depend on material appurtenances, but the value of these is scant unless they rest on the further moral factor of will. Fearful of Germany as they remained, the French did not consistently adhere to their initial policy of keeping Germany in impotence, yet at the same time they would not make the necessary concessions—perhaps impossible in any case—that would remove the grievances of Germany and of the other discontented powers of Europe. French policy between the wars is indeed open to criticism, though in some ways for the opposite reasons from those put forward at the time. The great failing of that policy lay in its unresolved ambiguity, which caused it in the end to make the worst of both worlds. It was symbolically appropriate that the cry "Why die for Danzig?" should on the eve of the Second World War have been uttered in France. As an expression of the collapse of the French policy and system none better could have been devised.

The collapse had in fact occurred some time before. It is usually situated quite correctly in 1936, when the French failed to make use of the last opportunity offered them, the German remilitarization of the Rhineland. The French thereafter, in abject fashion and to an unnecessary degree, surrendered their position to a British leadership that was, if anything, even less adequate than their own. But this is not the place to rehearse the familiar background of the last war or to attempt a further contribution to the weary debate on the merits of appeasement. In the present context the significance and the moral of it all is this: Britain and France, the former less obviously than the latter, had for some time been powers in positions of relative decline—this was the very fact which had brought them together before 1914—and they had won the war, but not alone, while the effort involved had in some ways injured them even more, France especially, than the hurt of defeat had injured a more vigorous Germany. We are dealing with one of Bismarck's imponderables, the factor of morale, will, or spirit. The fact is that neither Britain nor France was possessed of adequate power, including will, to effect an adequate reorganization of Europe. Thus victory itself was in some ways their greatest defeat. The fact that it served to conceal for a time the true reality of things was one of the aspects of the tragedy that the war had been for Europe.

2

The Retreat of Democracy

In default of British and French leadership, there were other candidates for the task. The new political systems which made their appearance after the First World War may all be lumped together under the label *totalitarian* because of the exaltation of the power of the state that characterizes them all. But within this common element there are important differences, and some distinctions must be drawn between the two main types, the Fascist and the Communist.

Here we come to an interesting situation, in which continuity with the past and severance from it are both manifest. The Allied victory, not omitting the American contribution, understandably redounded to the credit of democratic institutions. This fit to a nicety into the nineteenth-century wave, and victory was in part credited to the greater merits of governments controlled by the people, perhaps failing to give proper weight to the cruder factor of power. Still, it was undeniably true that the democracies had survived, their systems fundamentally unaltered, whereas the autocratic states had gone down, in their last stages swept by revolutions. After the war not only the new states but the defeated as well gave themselves constitutions patterned in the main on the British and French parliamentary models.

The success of the democratic idea rested on certain illusions. To assert the equal rights of men is one thing; to erect on that foundation an adequately functioning social and political order is an altogether different matter. Nothing is easier than for democracy to be corrupted and abused, and it contains in its very nature the seeds of its possible demise. It was not long before many of the new democratic regimes experienced difficulty in operating, since it is far easier for a parliament to hamper than to support the functioning of an administration. The interval between the two world wars witnessed the steady diminution of the area in which the democratic ordering prevailed.

Among notable instances of this retreat the Italian stands first, which is particularly important since Italy emerged from the war as one of the victors. Some indication has already been given of the stresses that the war had imposed on Italy and of the discontent and unrest prevalent in that country after the peace. On the one hand, the economic situation was very difficult, a consequence in part of the meagerness of Italian material resources; on the other, democracy and the parliamentary system lacked profound roots in the Italian tradition. For four years after the end of the war Italy jogged along, bedeviled by intense social stress, under the guidance of short-lived, ineffectual governments. Consultations of the people did not help; elections produced a large Socialist party and a similarly large new Catholic one, but the leadership of the two mass parties showed itself incapable of making the adjustments and compromises that would have been needed to keep the parliamentary system functioning. There was continuing talk and fear of the Red Bogey, exaggerated though it was, and the people were ready to accept short cuts and seemingly clearer solutions.

In September 1919, in the midst of the unproductive discussion of the Italian claims at the peace conference, the soldier-poet d'Annunzio seized the contested city of Fiume. That theatrical gesture, not of great significance in itself, was nonetheless an instance of successful insubordination that gave a measure of the weakness of the state. It was also in 1919, in Milan, that a movement which called itself Fascism was born. Its founder was none other than an ex-revolutionary Socialist leader, Benito Mussolini.

A general election, the first after the war, took place in Italy in November 1919. In preparation for it the Central Committee of the *Fasci* formulated the program of the party. It bears quoting as an illustration of the new tendencies that were abroad:

ITALIANS!
Here is the national program of a healthily Italian movement. This movement is revolutionary, because it is neither dogmatic nor demagogic; it is definitely new because unprejudiced.

It is our purpose to realize the value of the revolutionary war above all things and all people.

As to other problems, bureaucratic, administrative, judicial, educational, colonial, etc., we shall deal with them when we shall have created the ruling class.

In order to accomplish this we want:

For the political problem

(a) universal suffrage, with regional lists and proportional representation, and votes and eligibility for women.

(b) lowering of the voting age to 18; of eligibility for deputies to 25.

(c) abolition of the Senate.

(d) convocation of a national assembly for a period of three years, whose task it shall be to establish the form and constitution of the state.

(e) formation of national technical councils for labor, industry, social hygiene, communications, etc., elected by the professional groups and the trades, endowed with legal powers and with the right of electing a general commissioner with ministerial rank.

For the social problem we want:

(a) the immediate promulgation of a state law to establish the eight hour day for all workers.

(b) minimum wages.

(c) participation of workers' representatives in the technical management of industry.

(d) entrusting of these same proletarian organizations (when morally and technically worthy of it) with the management of industries and public services.

(e) rapid and complete organization of railway workers and all the transport industries.

(f) a necessary modification of the pending bill for disability and old age insurance, lowering the proposed age from 65 to 55.

For the military problem we want:

(a) institution of a national militia with short periods of instruction for exclusively defensive purposes.

(b) nationalization of all arms and explosives factories.

(c) a national foreign policy designed to give value in the world to the Italian nation in the peaceful competition of civilization.

For the financial problem we want:

(a) a heavy extraordinary tax on capital of progressive character that shall have the form of a real PARTIAL EXPROPRIATION of all wealth.

(b) confiscation of all the property of religious congregations and abolition of all episcopal allowances which constitute an enormous burden on the nation for the benefit of a few.

(c) revision of all contracts for war supplies and confiscation of 85 percent of war profits.

ITALIANS!

Italian Fascism in its new national life wants to continue to realize the value of the great soul fused and tempered in the great cement of war; it also wants to keep united—in the form of an anti-party or super-party—those Italians of all persuasions and of all the productive classes in order to sustain them in the new inevitable battles which must be fought to complete and realize the value of the great revolutionary war. The *Fasci di combattimento* want that the sum of sacrifices accomplished may give to Italians in international life that place which victory has assigned to them.

For this great work all must join the Italian *Fasci di combattimento.*

One will note at once the large socialist content of the Fascist program, qualified by the vaguely worded appeal to national union and pride contained in the peroration.

There was at first little response to the Fascist appeal, and Mussolini himself was ignominiously defeated in Milan. But in the midst of continuing disorder and unrest, to which the new movement itself contributed with its own tactics of violence, Fascism, promising order, made some progress. Not unimportant to its success was the failure of the state to maintain public order, interfering but little in the fights between the Fascist formations and the socialists.

By 1922 there were some thirty-five Fascist deputies in the Italian Chamber, a body of some five hundred men. It is a measure of the degree of decadence of the parliamentary institution in Italy that, in face of the inability of Parliament to produce a viable majority, Mussolini was called by the King to organize a government. With the freely given assent of Parliament, Mussolini thus became Prime Minister of Italy in October 1922. Of the legality of the act there could be no question, and there was in Italy in 1922 no feeling that a revolution had occurred, but we know the subsequent story of the Fascist regime in that country.

It is worth emphasizing, however, that Fascism offered an alternative to something which seemingly had failed. There were no new ideas in Fascism, yet it was an original synthesis, which the German name of the same product, National Socialism, expresses far better. Both nationalism and socialism had been well-entrenched and familiar components of the political landscape of Europe before 1914, but their reciprocal enmity was also a tradition. Fascism would not deny the rising mass and its claims, but for the validity of the class struggle was substituted the older, traditional one among nations. To emphasize the element of common interest on a national basis and to put stress on the legitimacy of the claims of the dispossessed and the poor, the "have-nots," against the satisfied "haves"—these, as fate would have it, were represented by the Western democracies —may seem a sleight of hand, an attempt to divert the social question into different channels, hence to confirm the existing social order—which to a point it was. Like it or no, and for all that the word has fallen in bad odor, there is no denying that Fascism is one of the important contributions to the political theory and practice of the twentieth century. Nor is it dead. Distortion though it may have been, it was definitely a product of the war, a response to conditions and circumstances that the war had in part created, in part merely accelerated in their evolution—in brief, a product of our time.

If the Italian case has the priority of model, the German turned out to be of greater importance. Hitler did not achieve in Germany the position of head of the government until 1933, but by that time the Nazi movement had taken far clearer shape than had Fascism in 1922.

Unlike Italy, Germany emerged from the war in unquestionable defeat, one consequence of which was a change in her regime. The advent of the Weimar Republic was the result of revolution, though the transition was relatively so smooth that some people were led to feel that what happened was confirmation of the congenital inability of the German people to effect a revolution. The new regime seemed to become consolidated and to give proof of the successful spread of democracy, however pedestrian its operation and its leadership may have been.

Nevertheless, in Germany also the authority of the state had been challenged. In Berlin the prospects of a Communist take-over imme-

diately after the war were promptly seen to be an illusion, though
it took some bloodshed to establish the fact. But Bavaria was for a
time under Communist rule. The regime was short lived, but it is
significant that in bringing about its downfall irregular military
formations played an important role; the *Freikorps* bears some resemblance to the freebooters whom d'Annunzio led into Fiume.
The *Freikorps,* for that matter, also played a role in the chaos that
prevailed in the Baltic countries, whence it was only evicted with
some difficulty.

These challenges to the authority of the state might seem to be
passing manifestations of illness in the body politic. But they were
not. For if order was apparently restored in Germany, its foundation
was too fragile. The attempted *Putsch* in 1923 in Munich, in which
both Hitler and Ludendorff participated, collapsed amid ridicule
at the time, and the weird lucubrations of *Mein Kampf* that Hitler
penned in the seclusion of his subsequent imprisonment did not
seem to deserve the attention of sane and serious men.

As long as Germany prospered the Nazis remained on the fringe
—the lunatic fringe, many thought—of the political spectrum. But
as soon as conditions became difficult again their progress was as
rapid as it was alarming; the election of September 1930 raised their
membership in the Reichstag from 12 to 107; within another two
years their deputies numbered 230. When he finally achieved power,
Hitler, like Mussolini, posed as the savior and the restorer of order;
both men demanded unfettered power to achieve their end, but the
supposedly transitional period turned into permanency of tenure,
while the formerly existing "order" was changed beyond recognition.

The state became all powerful, controlling and directing all aspects of the activity of the individual. Opposition was ruthlessly
suppressed, and it was wholly appropriate that with both pride and
glee the demise of democracy should be proclaimed. The aberrations of Nazism are sufficiently known, its extraordinary racial doctrine in particular, but if Italy was spared for the most part that
special form of insanity, the similarity between the two regimes is
otherwise striking. Both professed to be dedicated to saving European civilization from Bolshevik barbarism, a task that decadent
democracies were incapable of performing.

Limited as the appeal of National Socialism may have been by the stress it placed on the claim to national superiority, its example was nonetheless contagious, which is perhaps not too surprising if one considers that some of its other aspects suited the uncertain conditions that existed in many of the new states. As time passed, from Austria to Rumania and from the Baltic to the Adriatic, all fell under more or less dictatorial regimes, until Czechoslovakia alone survived as a state that could still be called democratic. Everyone is familiar with what happened in Spain, whose governance could be called democratic only for a brief spell and by courtesy, even before Franco established control. We need not dwell on Portugal. Even in France, the Continental home of the democratic idea, the examples of what went on across the Alps and the Rhine had some impact. In Britain, in some small Northern countries, and in Switzerland alone did it appear that democracy would continue to function unchallenged. In the United States, where resources are immense and the tradition of government has solid roots, even the Great Depression offered no significant challenge to the political system. But clearly, one of the great consequences of the war was to raise the question of the validity of the democratic idea and practice.

Even clearer was the challenge that had arisen during the war itself from the Russian quarter. The Bolshevik regime rested on the well-established and familiar Marxist interpretation of society and of history. This may be granted greater depth and consistency as a philosophical foundation than any to be found in the jumble of National Socialist thought. It was entirely appropriate that Communists and Fascists should become seemingly irreconcilable enemies and hurl vituperation, when no worse, at each other. But this is also misleading superficial appearance; opposite extremes as they seemed to be, one is reminded of the observation that *les extrêmes se touchent.*

It has been pointed out, a phenomenon most clearly perceived in the case of Italian Fascism, that the system took shape gradually and as a response and adaptation to circumstances. In the domain of practical affairs, in the actual practice of government, existing conditions are always paramount; government and politics are practical pursuits of the art of the possible that can bend theory at least as much as they themselves are shaped by more abstract considerations. Once Lenin and his Bolsheviks were in control of the Russian state, obviously their first task was to survive, and very soon it appeared that the egalitarian communist millennium must be put off for some time. Since consultation of the Russian people failed to produce an amenable representation, the simple radical solution was to dismiss that which issued from the first election. It was an easy step from this to asserting that the direction of the Russian state and the governance of the Russian people must remain firmly in the hands of the competently qualified, meaning by this the Bolshevik leadership. The proletariat, through the Communist party, must exercise dictatorship, and the Communist party meant an essentially self-appointed leadership.

There was in the Communist case less pretense than in the Fascist, in the sense that while the latter endeavored to enroll the mass, the former adopted a far more restrictive practice. The Communist party in the Soviet Union remained a selected élite whose ranks were not easy to enter. But in effect the difference was not as great as might appear from these divergent practices, for in both cases controls were firmly clenched by the top leadership, the emergence of which was the result of the interplay of forces and personalities within a very narrow circle. The struggle at the center could be harsh, and the stakes physical existence itself, but once the issue had been resolved rigid discipline prevailed. There could be in such regimes no room for free, open discussion at the popular level, or for a free press. The latter was instead avowedly annexed as an instrument of indoctrination, "education" in more polite parlance. Thus the totalitarian systems emerged, in a way harking back to a supposedly dead past, with the important difference, however, that the twentieth-century totalitarian state commanded the powerful resources of twentieth-century technique.

In the Russian case the leadership of Lenin was freely accepted within the Bolshevik group, and it was only after his passing that inner struggles for control ensued, but the bloody record of their unfolding, often a tax on credibility and the imagination, need not detain us. Lenin was the all-powerful dictator of the Soviet state, rather more powerful in fact than his predecessors, Autocrats of all the Russias. Able, intelligent, dedicated, and strong-willed, Lenin had first to come to terms with reality. The peace of Brest-Litovsk did not bring peace to Russia, but worsening chaos instead, which reduced her to incredible misery and primitiveness and set her economic development an appreciable distance back. However, the combination of inefficiency, bungling, and weariness on the part of the anti-Bolsheviks, both domestic and foreign, plus on the other side ruthlessness in the service of an idea, resulted in a stalemate where both the Revolution and the outside, unconverted capitalist world could survive. This was theoretically incorrect, for the impossibility of simultaneous survival of the two was about the only point of agreement between the opposing sides. But facts are facts, and Lenin would have been the last to deny them. Behind the *cordon sanitaire,* dike as well as protecting wall, Russia proceeded to rebuild and reorganize from the very bottom.

The successful modernization of Russia, at least in technical terms, was to be the accomplishment of the succeeding decades. It has been argued that even without war and revolution, as far as economic development goes Russia would be today more or less at the point where she is. On the other hand, it has been contended that the Communist dictatorship deserves the sole credit for the modernization of Russia, and comparisons have been made between the cost in hardship to the Russian people and the sufferings that the coming of industry brought to the people of Britain, for example, over a longer time and at a slower pace. This is an interesting speculation, though a debate incapable of resolution. More relevant in this discussion are two things.

It appears that the similarities between the various totalitarian systems, Red, Black, or Brown, are considerable. They may all be regarded as adaptations and responses to conditions that the war did not actually create but the development of which it rather accelerated and sharpened. In the face of vastly larger and fast-proliferating numbers, in the face also of the rapid developments of technique, the question has to be faced of how to organize and operate a modern society. In the more advanced states democracies and parliaments have taken root, together with a tradition of freedom, whatever may be the interconnections, causal or otherwise, between the two developments. The less advanced have resorted to short cuts, which in the context of their past experience have confirmed and strengthened the old tradition of the strong state. This continuity of development, however, has had the effect of breaking what, prior to and for a short time after the war, seemed to be the inescapable tide of the rising wave of democracy.

But even in the more advanced states, where democratic institutions have remained unchallenged, the inevitable response has been a vast increase of the powers of the state, that not a few view with concern. The peaceful emergence of the welfare state may be an adequate answer to the totalitarian challenge, and it may be that once the underdeveloped have caught up in material development they will by a different road return to the search to find scope for the unquenchable human yearning for freedom. This is one of the great posers of the present that the future will answer; incidentally, it contains interesting food for thought and material for the debate on the validity of the Marxist analysis. But it may be regarded as established that numbers and technique alone will insure a very large place to the role of the central power. Also, it is quite clear that general awareness of the problem has in large part been induced as a consequence of what happened during the First World War, even though the clear recognition and formulation of it have required some time.

Secondly, and this applies especially to the Communist Revolution, we have had, as a result of that event, a situation that bears some resemblance to that which resulted from the French Revolution at the end of the eighteenth century. By contrast with the starry-eyed naïveté of eighteenth-century Utopian thinkers, twentieth-century Marxists think themselves sophisticated and "scientific." They have given much time and care to the study of the French Revolution and to the episode of the Parisian Commune, with an eye to learning the lessons of their failures. Lenin and his followers were hard, realistic men, highly respectful of the ways of power. Yet it is well to bear in mind that the eighteenth-century Utopians were strongly influenced by the scientific accomplishment of their own time, the Newtonian synthesis above all. If their worship of Reason may seem to us somewhat naïve, it was rooted in belief in the possibilities of the rational faculty, and this is implied in any scientific endeavor. There is here an important point of contact between earlier and latter-day social reformers. For, granting the refinements of technique, the technique of revolution included, the element of faith remains a powerful component of the Marxist appeal, however great its professed scorn of other faiths. Thus Communism has in a sense been quite right in its insistence on the exclusiveness of party membership. It is not meant for the mass, which, however, in part from its dissatisfaction with the past and the present, in part from its hope in future promise, may provide support for the Communist Utopia. It is significant that in conditions of free choice the Communists have obtained strong support in such countries as Czechoslovakia, Italy, and France—incidentally, countries in which the Catholic influence is also strong. A large number of these supporters have little knowledge, if any, of the content and nature of the Marxist doctrine; their response is compounded of discontent and faith. And it is wholly appropriate that the leadership of the movement, the early leadership especially, none more than Marx and Lenin themselves, should have been made up of typical bourgeois intellectuals. Only recently has some of the Communist leadership emerged from the ranks of the authentic workers.

The great surge of Communist success is characteristic of the post Second World War period. This is in part the result of the crude assertion of Soviet power, but far more significant is the extent of the real response that Communism has commanded without the support of Russian arms. Circumstances foiled the Soviet hope of world revolution after the First World War, and for the major part of the interval between the wars the Soviet Union lived in comparative isolation, attending to the necessary domestic reconstruction. These same circumstances and those that followed have resulted in considerable distortion of and deviation from the initial prophecies and expectations, for Russia, Marxist or otherwise, continued to endure as a state among states. In a broad sense, that situation is also reminiscent of the period after the outbreak of the French Revolution. Europe, let alone the world, was not immediately converted to the French example, and France continued to exist as a state among states, behaving very much as France. Nevertheless, the seeds planted in 1789 prospered, until by the time of the First World War many of the fundamental principles of the French upheaval had been accepted by all; there was by 1914 nothing very revolutionary about the prospect of universal suffrage, for example. During the first half of the nineteenth century it was said that "when Paris catches cold Europe sneezes." Moscow may be substituted for Paris, and the world for Europe, in our time. One of the things that makes the Russian Revolution so acceptable to many people is that it appears to them as an extension of the uncompleted task of the French. To Americans, the sharp awareness of the Russian threat, either as ideology or power, is in large part a phenomenon that followed the Second World War, but the real break took place during the First, just as a real break occurred in 1789, however much the old order may have ostensibly been restored in 1815. Quite understandably, the awareness of the change was sharper in Europe, and Communism after the First World War was an important factor in the politics of the Continent.

3

The Changed Place of Europe in the World

One reason for the more limited impact of the Russian Revolution in the United States lay in the economic condition of America, where much that Communism stood for had little significance. Even the Great Depression did no more than induce a greater degree of sympathetic interest and understanding among some intellectuals, brain trusters, and New Dealers, but none that mattered in the mass. The view that the Roosevelt administration was part of the great Communist plot has been the appanage of the lunatic fringe. But there was for this lack of response another reason as well—the simple fact of power.

When France embarked on revolution, and under Napoleon set about conquering Europe, she was the most advanced as well as the most powerful state of the Continent. She was still so after 1815. In contrast, Russia in 1917 was, among major states, the most backward; nor, whatever her unrealized potential might eventually develop into, was she then and for some appreciable time thereafter possessed of substantial power. Where power is concerned the contrast between 1815 France and 1920 Russia is striking. Something has already been said on the subject, and the consequences have been noted of a situation where one of the great states of Europe had totally ceased to exist while two others were powerless, with the corollary of placing French power in a false, indeed an absurd and impossible, position.

This very situation has been the source of comparisons between the settlement of Vienna and that contrived in Paris, often to the detriment of the latter. There is some point to this critical appraisal, but the difference is not so much due to the greater wisdom or ability of the statesmen of Vienna as to the very nature of the First World War; this element has also been explained. The expectation after 1919 was that sometime, somehow, Germany and Russia would

159

be reintegrated to a commensurate place in the European community. Indeed, certain steps were taken in that direction: in 1926 Germany became a member of the League of Nations, and Russia did likewise in 1934. But these were hesitant steps rather than radical changes. Germany remained subject to many disabilities—disarmament, for example—and foreign suspicion of the Soviet Union abated but little.

The Demotion of Europe

The war had in effect destroyed beyond retrieving the political structure of Europe. The appellation *superpower* has been in favor since the Second World War, when there are supposed to be just two such; it would have been equally valid after the First World War when there was only one. The uniqueness of the American position of power was a fact that none could deny, one that the precipitate dismantling of the American war machine did not alter. The British raised no difficulty about accepting parity of naval power with the United States, thereby showing intelligent acceptance of their own demotion, yet even parity was not in correspondence with the true measure of relative power, but history has certain claims and there was no desire on the American side to insist upon recognition of place beyond a certain point.

But here the earlier-mentioned contrast between the American and the European view of things must be recalled. It was indeed possible for the United States to recover the sense of a return to "normalcy." Yet it was illusion, for once American power had been brought to bear upon the course of world affairs, with decisive effects, retreat from the consequences was impossible. However much isolation may have been cherished and believed to have been recovered, the attempted abstention from action had effects that were other, but not less, than those of willing positive participation. For that matter, even abstention was a qualified condition. The new tariff of 1922, if designed to protect America from competition, was also a highly positive act. By reducing the facility of commercial exchanges, it magnified and exacerbated the problem of the discharge of the world's debt to America.

The war had brusquely changed America from a debtor to an almost universal creditor. We shall not mention again the curious aberration whereby America financed for a time the payment to herself of foreign obligations, meanwhile increasing their total. The fact that this happened, however, is clear measure of the commanding place of the United States in the world's economy and finances. The comparative figures of production, consumption, and income all tell the same tale of the truly unique and gigantic proportions of the American economy. It was a strange situation indeed where there was one power on earth whose position towered so far above all others that the concept of a collectivity of roughly equal great powers had lost its old significance.

For the other great powers the sense of relative demotion could not be denied. Europe recovered from the war, and even, for a brief space, barely the second half of the twenties, could enjoy the illusion of prosperity. She strove to recapture lost markets, and in general her former position, but it was no longer possible to maintain that she was the mistress and the power house of the planet. Even though the recognition of this altered place was not fully brought home before another suicidal conflict had again ravaged Europe, there was more than the rise of America to furnish evidence of the diminution of Europe.

The British had emerged from the war, as usual, with enlarged imperial possessions. They could take particular satisfaction in having closed the gap between the Indian Ocean and Suez as a result of the paramount place they had achieved in the intervening Arab world. This pleasing illusion was very short lived; as early as 1922 the resurgence of Turkey and the corresponding defeat of the Greeks was a major setback to Britain's Near Eastern position. Britain did not react with very great vigor, and if her lenient attitude in dealing with the Arab world may be seen as a manifestation of flexible adaptability to changing conditions, it was evidence as well that British power and the British position had changed. The Arab world was not content, and the path of concessions would have but one terminal point, full independence. Nor could the British handle the dragons' teeth that began to sprout in Palestine. Albeit not until 1947, Britain had finally to acknowledge that this particular task was beyond her capability to cope with.

It was mentioned above that mandates were divided into three categories, corresponding to the degree of political, economic, and social development of the peoples in them. It was by this criterion appropriate that "A" Mandates should appear among the Arab people, in Syria and Iraq, for example. These had been part of the Ottoman Empire. Large segments of the Turkish core of the empire had been allotted to the victors as spheres of influence, and there was even passing thought of an Armenian and a Kurdish state, while the zone of the Straits was to be internationalized. What happened in Turkey deserves attention as harbinger of a broad trend and of larger subsequent developments.

From the group of patriotic Turks, resentful of the decadence long familiar to their state, there arose one, Kemal, who would not accept the final humiliation registered in the Treaty of Sèvres. As early as 1919 Kemal set out for Anatolia, where he began organizing resistance as well as laying the foundations of Turkish rebirth. In January 1920 an assembly of sorts proclaimed in Ankara the Nationalist Pact, which rates in modern Turkish annals a place comparable to that held by the Declaration of Independence in the American story. Kemal was successful. Dealing first with the Italians and the French, who soon came to terms, then with the luckless Greeks, the Turks secured the Treaty of Lausanne in 1923, undoing for Turkey proper the effects of the settlement of 1920, the Kurds and the Armenians having meantime been forgotten.

Here was nevertheless a prime example of the penetration of European influence, for Kemal definitely turned to the West for a model of the new Turkish institutions, even to making the state secular, a bold and major step in the Muslim milieu. His outlook and his work have rightly been compared to those of Tsar Peter I, down to the seemingly humorous but far from insignificant matter of dress. Operating in the twentieth rather than in the eighteenth century, Kemal introduced parliamentary institutions, but in effect he was, like Tsar Peter, an enlightened and ruthless dictator. The title of Ataturk, "father of the Turks," bestowed upon him by a grateful people, he well deserved for his successful leadership of the Turkish bid for independence.

But although he was paying the West the homage of acknowledging its superior advancement, he did this in revolt against Western control. Nationalism, that other typical product of the West,
had been effectively transferred to the Turks. But at the same time
nationalist Turkey did a wise thing in abandoning any dreams of
empire; Turkey, allowing for the Armenian and Kurdish qualifications, was henceforth to be Turkish. The Arabs would have to look
after themselves, and for them the Treaty of Sèvres retained its
validity.

But if the Arabs had risen against Turkish control during the
war, it was not for the purpose of substituting another master, and
the Turkish example was infectious. There have been in the Arab
world many candidates for a role comparable to that of Kemal, but
all so far have failed; the record of the most successful to date, the
Egyptian Nasser, is still in the making. The twentieth-century record of the Arab world has been troubled and tortuous and does not
belong in this treatment. Its efforts to emerge into modernity have
been beset by the stresses arising from a real but loose unity deriving
from its common culture and the Islamic religion, in contrast to
secular tendencies and the very unequal degree of development of
the separate Arab nations, some of them still feudal in structure.
But the thread has run clear since the First World War, the great
turning point in the essentially successful Arab struggle for emancipation from Europe's imperial control, one of the major instances
of the retreat and demotion of Europe initiated by that conflict.

The retreat of imperial control is frequently regarded as desirable, and the acceptance of it by the imperial powers of Europe may
be seen as a manifestation of intelligence or virtue; it is in any case
a clear indication of diminished power. Not the least significant
aspect of it—especially in the cases of Britain and France, the two
great imperial powers most affected—is the loss of the aggressive
and dominating will that has occurred at home. There were, for a
brief time, seemingly vigorous manifestations of imperial ambition
in Italy, which even conquered Abyssinia. Apart from the fact that
much of the Italian performance was paper tiger bombast, the short-
lived Italian victory, by helping precipitate another European war,
accelerated the final termination of Europe's imperial position.

In actual fact the retreat of the imperial position of Europe between the two world wars was not substantial. But what really matters is that the war itself greatly accelerated the growth of the seeds of independence that European conquest had brought in its baggage. The ultimate outcome may be regarded as inevitable in any event, and Europe's imperial position as one that could in any case have been no more than a passage. The point is that the First World War was the crucial turning point in the process to which the Second World War gave but the final *coup de grâce*. By now it is not only the Arabs who have freed themselves from European domination; in the whole of Asia and in Africa what still remains of European empires amounts to no more than tatters and remnants. There are few instances in history of so sharp and abrupt a reversal.

The Attempt at World Organization

The United States has been generally sympathetic, at times un-critically so, to the struggle for independence of the peoples subject to Europe's control. Save in so far as America's economic power has tended to intrude into Europe's colonial domain, and to some de-gree even to displace European dominance, American support of independence has been at once authentic and consistent. It was America's gift to the world that took the shape of the League of Nations. Undeniably, the League had been a failure, and for that reason need not be dwelt upon at length. America's denial of her own child was clearly an important fact that may, conceivably, have made the difference between success and failure of the world or-ganization. The League did many useful things, though of a minor nature, and for a brief time, coincident with the return of favorable economic conditions and the admission of Germany, the League became the focus of high hopes, while Geneva began to look like the world's capital, where Briand's speeches evoked a wide and en-thusiastic response, to which Stresemann more cautiously responded in kind.

But even in its heyday the League was incapable of achieving two things. Its primary purpose of insuring world peace was closely linked with the problem of disarmament, or at least the control and the limitation of armaments. The difficulty lay in the fact that the dilemma between security and disarmament proved impossible of resolution. The French were at the time the chief defenders—the chief villains some thought—of the position: we shall disarm, and gladly, as soon as and to the extent that means other than our own shall provide for our security. This has become the present American position, and the current discussions of disarmament have a very familiar ring. The logic of that position is irrefutable, but it runs into the other difficulty that the League, like the United Nations, was incapable of resolving—the inescapable necessity of organizing a system that will insure the safety of all. For such a system implies the willingness, so far lacking among the great powers, to surrender at least in part the attribute of sovereignty.

The heyday of the League was short. When it came face to face with the issue of curbing the action of a major state, the Japanese aggression in Manchuria, its impotence was exposed. Japan's success was followed by her withdrawal from the world organization.

Some still found comfort in the explanation of special circumstances, mainly the absence of the United States and of the Soviet Union, which impeded action in the Far East, and thought that the League might still successfully function in the European context. But Germany quit the League almost simultaneously with Japan, and her replacement in it by the Soviet Union had rather more to do with considerations of power than with the professed aim of world order. Italy, unquestionably a European power, sealed the fate of the League with her Abyssinian adventure; thereafter, crude considerations of power alone guided the policies of states. The Axis, the most immediately active agent of change, succeeded in its aim of destroying the existing international order, even though the final outcome was to entail its own destruction as well.

Despite its failure, the experiment was of the highest importance. For this was the first time in man's history when a formal attempt had been made to create universal order on a basis other than the existence of predominant power in any one quarter. Optimistically, one may see the attempt as a manifestation of the rising moral purpose of mankind; more modestly, it can be interpreted as a lesson of the experience of the First World War, consisting in the acceptance of the view that war is not the proper way to settle differences in a presumably civilized society. That view stands in contrast to the one which sees war as an instrument of progress—a view, incidentally, not to be lightly dismissed. At the very least, war is a powerful promoter of change. The most recent world war certainly induced, or at least accelerated, vast technical transformations. This alone, most specifically because of advances in weaponry, would suffice to give greater urgency and validity to the 1914 belief that guns were too powerful for the actual use of them to be conceivable. Thus we are in the midst of a repetition of the attempt to create order that was born of the First World War. The United Nations, like the League, has been a useful instrument that has, however, not conclusively succeeded in keeping order among the great powers. But since they have not, at this writing, fallen out among themselves in open violence, the United Nations may not yet be said to have either failed or succeeded.

4

The Second Thirty Years War

Since the First World War had such a great impact on Europe, it may be appropriate in closing these pages to cast a brief glance at the contemporary record of Europe. The point has been made that the war destroyed the traditional structure of Europe. Yet enough survived of the past—the destruction, if one will, was not sufficiently thorough—so that it was for a time possible to cherish the illusion of continuity and recapture of the past. At the same time, that past had been sufficiently maimed not to be able to recover its vitality. Thus the war left Europe amid much unfinished business, with the consequence that the two decades of the long armistice were in the main an uninspiring passage of fumbling search for a stability that could not be recovered merely by turning back. The victors lacked the will, if not perhaps the power; the discontented vanquished would not rest until they had encompassed the downfall of the victors; while everywhere the mass, some of it looking to the Muscovite beacon for guidance, was pressing for greater recognition of its place and its rights.

The Second World War has finished the uncompleted task of the first and has had a greatly clarifying effect. Among the European participants all save Britain and Russia were in one way or another defeated. And even Britain, although her role was the most inspiring of any, suffered in a sense the same fate. As in the case of France in the preceding conflict, the cost of victory was for Britain too great. The war left Europe, not excluding Russia, a shambles.

Leaving Russia aside, the war thus completed the demotion of Europe to a degree that none could fail to acknowledge. One consequence of this has been the termination of the imperial power of Europe. There are few parallels in history, if any, for the record of the past hundred years in the imperial domain. During that interval Europe conquered the planet, or at least completed that task at an extraordinarily rapid pace. After a hesitant passage between the two wars, the dam of independence suddenly broke after 1945, with consequences even more sensational than those of the imperial conquest. It is difficult to exaggerate the significance and the magnitude of this development that some regard as *the* most important of all.

This catastrophic change might be taken as confirmation of the popular view that Europe was truly finished, again with the Soviet exception. Yet it has not been a catastrophe. For, after a fairly brief postwar continuation of wartime misery, Europe recovered in a fashion that has been as astounding as it was unexpected. There is no need to go into comparative details of different conditions, or to seek to establish which "miracle" has been the most miraculous. The recovery in its clearest form has been economic, and Europe's production now far exceeds that of the last prewar period. Amid widespread prosperity, and to the accompaniment of a rapid rate of expansion, the welfare state has come to all, giving unprecedented recognition to the claims of the common man. Recovery and growth have come to the Soviet Union as well, though that country still has some appreciable distance to travel before achieving the standard of more highly developed states. Interestingly, recovery has been relatively laggard in Britain, the other European victor in the war.

But most surprising of all, Europe has reacted vigorously to the loss of her position. For the first time since the days of Roman unity, the never wholly abandoned dream of the recovery of that unity is showing signs of emerging into the domain of the concrete and the possible. Precisely because Europe finds herself just Europe, no longer mistress of the world—in fact in some respects the object of external pressures—she has developed a greater consciousness of the virtues and of the need of unity. In the larger context of the world as a whole, the emphasis indeed may be placed on those elements that make for distinction between the totality of Europe and the rest, elements of similarity best summed up under the heading of common culture. If we bear in mind the importance of the ancient legacies of Greece and of Rome, to which that of Christianity may be added, the sum total of these influences appears as impressive and considerable. Perhaps one should recall the days when Islam threatened Europe, a danger which led to a consciousness of unity and at least some cooperation.

The fact that Europe has for some centuries developed so much power, power in the broad sense that includes guns as well as ideas, and that she conquered and shaped the whole modern world, enabled her to give full scope to those elements of diversity that constitute so great a part of her richness. The modern state system made up of separate sovereignties was the result. Into this mold nationalism was poured and then ran riot. From one standpoint the First World War may be regarded as an explosion resulting from the fact that there was too much power in Europe, more than her exiguous bounds could contain. The exaltation of nationalism that attended the outbreak of that conflict is something that is becoming difficult to understand. The outcome of that war in its settlements registered the high point of the nationalistic force, but it also established that that same force could have suicidal effects.

Perhaps as much from instinctive reaction as from clear analytical examination, Europe seems to have felt that the recoil from suicide implied the abandonment of the worship of the nation as the supreme value. Nationalism is anything but dead, but Europe is no longer the place to observe its more virulent manifestations. A very startling illustration, as well as one seemingly unthinkable but a short time ago, may be found in the altered climate of the Franco-German relationship; not only are the formal aspects of that relationship very different from what they were after the First World War, but more important, the tone of it has changed at the grass roots level as well. It is certainly significant that one of the most convinced French propounders of the new relationship should be the very man who, during the last war, was the embodiment of resistance to the Germany of Hitler.

This raises some very interesting questions. It may be granted that the core of any unity in Europe lies in the Franco-German combination. But there is a good deal more to Europe besides these two nations. The question is, how much, or in different words, precisely what and where is Europe? There was, immediately after the last war, a movement for European union, but it failed to capture the imagination of the European peoples. However, once physical recovery had been achieved, the decade of the fifties witnessed some more concrete achievements. A number of ideas, in the initiation of which the French have had a large though not exclusive share, have borne fruit. The names of Schuman and Monnet among the French stand out, to which those of Adenauer in Germany and of de Gasperi in Italy should be added, to mention but a few. The organization of the Coal and Steel Community was the first step, sensibly beginning at the level of limited economic aims, though larger political goals are at the root of the thought of the would-be makers of Europe. By 1957 the Treaty of Rome had been signed, creating the Little Europe of the Six: France, West Germany, Italy, and the Benelux countries—the Common Market. France was the most hesitant member of the association at first, but her economic recovery and the final liquidation of her imperial problem destroyed her reservations, and the association has been highly beneficial to all.

Even the Europe of the Six, reminiscent of Charlemagne's empire, is but a fraction of Europe. Under the leadership of Britain another combination, the European Free Trade Association, consisting of seven members,[1] was organized. Of the two the Common Market has been the greater success, but it was inevitable that the thought of the possibility of merging the two groups should arise. In doing this the main problem lies in finding an accommodation between the British and the Six. This is understandably difficult, for the British on their side are torn between divergent attractions (Europe of the Continent, the Commonwealth, America)—in other words, are faced with the problem of making a drastic readjustment to their individually diminished position. It is a hard choice, and on the Continental side, especially in France, suspicion of Albion survives. The issue at this writing remains unresolved.

The Six and the Seven, even in combination, leave out the Soviet empire, consisting of the Soviet Union itself and her Eastern European satellites. The contemporary Cold War is a contest between two coalitions led respectively by the United States and the Soviet Union, the two great superpowers of the day. It would take us too far afield and exceed the bounds of this treatment to embark upon a discussion of the development of the Communist world. At one extreme lies the view of irreconcilable difference, perhaps most

---

[1] The European Free Trade Association is made up, in addition to Britain, of Sweden, Norway, Denmark, Portugal, Switzerland, and Austria. There has been a tendency to enlarge the original groupings, especially the Common Market, by giving others associate status, as in the case of Greece, for example.

neatly summed up in ex-Chairman Khrushchev's phrase, "We shall bury you." But much has been happening in the Communist world during the past fifteen years. The possibility has been indicated that the impact of the Russian Revolution might be absorbed and integrated into the larger stream of development in the same way as that of the French Revolution was absorbed during the nineteenth century (for a long time the word *republic* has not frightened any one). Also, the emergence of Communism in China has raised some problems whose solution is still not clear. Putting these last two observations together, there may be a point in recalling General de Gaulle's view that Europe extends to the Urals and that the Russian Revolution is a passage of adjustment.

Then there is the United States, which undoubtedly belongs with the West. The United States, with combined generosity and wisdom, vastly contributed to the recovery of Europe. It has been the chief organizer of the anti-Soviet coalition and has been sympathetic to the prospect of European integration. Quite understandably, and on the whole quite rightly also, the United States has thought primarily in terms of defense. Beyond this, there has been some discussion of the Grand Design of an Atlantic Community, rooted in the common cultural tradition of the West. There seems to be no visible cause for clash between the two sides of the Atlantic, any more than there has been between America and Britain, which have instead acknowledged a broad community of interest.

But it may also be pointed out that America was originally born to independence in revolt against Britain. There is too much in Europe, especially if united, for the whole to accept for long a relationship of subservience to America, or to anyone else. Thus, what may seem to be ingratitude must be accepted as a normal, indeed a healthy, development. Very likely what is taking place under our very eyes is the passing of the short-lived dominance of two superpowers, in place of which may emerge a more fragmented distribution of power among a greater number of centers. The realization and the consequences of such a possibility belong in the future.

The preceding discussion may seem unrelated to the significance of an event that took place half a century ago. Yet it is not. The phrase *Second Thirty Years War* has been used to describe the period that encloses the two world wars of our time. The two indeed form a unit, separated by the long armistice, during which the Old Order unsuccessfully strove to re-establish control but was unable to do so. In the fumbling ways of mankind another conflict ensued to complete the unfinished task of the first. It was the first great war that irretrievably undermined the Old Order when Europe had given the whole world its modern shape while imposing her mastery upon it. It was the First World War that opened the way to realizing the forecasts made by de Tocqueville about America and Russia. The fact of American power was definitely established in 1919, even if the American people sought to recoil from its implications; not until the Second World War did Soviet power achieve comparable status. It was the First World War that laid the bases for the rebellion of the dependent peoples; in this case also the dormant seed finally sprouted only after the second conflict. Finally, and perhaps most important of all, it was the First World War that broke the dyke of the nineteenth-century social structure; the claims of the Common Man for recognition could no longer be denied. Yet neither the Wilsonian New Order nor that which Lenin envisaged have succeeded in creating universal order and peace. The problems of mankind are never so much solved as the mold in which they are cast alters its shape. No one should be surprised to find that our time is beset by deep uncertainty and bedeviling confusion. The scientific and technical explosion is no less a source of stress than the population explosion, and the current state of literature and the arts is apt expression of the search for an answer to unresolved dilemmas. But on whatever clouded course we may be launched, no one now thinks of going back to the days of 1939, let alone those of pre-1914. The First World War was the great break with the past. That is its fundamental meaning.

Bibliography

The literature about the First World War is vast. In the following list no more is attempted than to offer some useful suggestions to the reader who may be interested in pursuing some aspects of the conflict. A number of the books listed themselves contain more ample bibliographies. An attempt has been made to give titles that deal with a variety of approaches: political, social, economic, military, diplomatic, etc. A number of very recent publications are included that deal with specific and limited episodes; they reflect the current revival of interest in the first great conflict of our century. A few titles are fiction; such are at times more effective than sedate scholarly works in conveying the spirit and the flavor of a time.

Albertini, Luigi, *The Origins of the War of 1914,* 3 vols. (1953-1957). This is the most complete and best balanced diplomatic history.

Albrecht-Carrié, René, *A Diplomatic History of Europe Since the Congress of Vienna* (1958).

Angell, Norman, *The Great Illusion* (1911, reprinted 1933).

Arthur, Sir George, *The Memoirs of Raymond Poincaré,* 2 vols. (1935).

Asquith, Herbert H., *The Genesis of the War* (1923).

Bailey, Thomas A., *Wilson and the Peacemakers,* 2 vols. in 1 (1947).

Barbusse, Henri, *Under Fire* (1917).

Barnett, Correlli, *The Swordbearers: Supreme Command in the First World War* (1964).

Bethmann-Hollweg, Theobald von, *Reflections on the World War* (1920).

Birdsall, Paul, *Versailles Twenty Years After* (1941).

Chamberlin, William H., *The Russian Revolution,* 2 vols. (1935).

Chambers, Frank P., *The War Behind the War, 1914-1918* (1939).

Churchill, Winston S., *The World Crisis,* 4 vols. in 5 (1923-1929).

Cole, G. D. H., *The Second International, 1889-1914,* 2 vols. (1956).

Cruttwell, C. R. M. F., *A History of the Great War, 1914-1918* (1934).

Del Corral, Luis Diez, *The Rape of Europe* (1959).

Falls, Cyril, *The Great War, 1914-1918* (1959).

————, *Armageddon: 1918* (1964).

Fay, Sidney B., *The Origins of the World War*, 2 vols. in 1 (1932).

Feis, Herbert, *Europe: the World's Banker, 1870-1914* (1936).

Gatzke, Hans W., *Germany's Drive to the West* (1950).

Graves, Robert, *Goodbye to All That* (1957).

Horne, Alistair, *The Price of Glory, Verdun 1916* (1962).

Hughes, H. Stuart, *Consciousness and Society: The Reorientation of European Social Thought, 1890-1930* (1958).

Kennan, George F., *Russia Leaves the War* (1956).

Keynes, John Maynard, *The Economic Consequences of the Peace* (1920).

King, Jere C., *Generals and Politicians* (1951).

Lawrence, T. E., *Seven Pillars of Wisdom* (1935).

————, *Revolt in the Desert* (1927).

Liddell Hart, B. H., *The War in Outline* (1936).

————, *The Real War, 1914-1918* (reprinted 1964).

Mansergh, Nicholas, *The Coming of the First World War* (1949).

Maurice, Frederick B., *The Armistices of 1918* (1939).

Mayer, Arno, *Political Origins of the New Diplomacy* (1959).

Mendelssohn-Bartholdy, A., *The War and German Society* (1938).

Meyer, Henry Cord, *Mitteleuropa in German Thought and Action* (1958).

Montgelas, Max, *The Case for the Central Powers* (1925).

Moorehead, Alan, *Gallipoli* (1956).

Nicolson, Harold, *Peacemaking 1919* (1933).

Paxson, Frederic L., *American Democracy and the First World War*, 3 vols. (1936-1948).

Pitt, Barrie, *1918: The Last Act* (1962).

Pribam, Alfred F., *England and the International Policy of the European Great Powers, 1871-1914* (1931).

Remarque, Erich Maria, *All Quiet on the Western Front* (1929).

Renouvin, Pierre, *The Immediate Origins of the War* (1928).

Romains, Jules, *Verdun* (Vol. VIII of "Men of Good Will") (1940).

Rudin, Harry, *Armistice 1918* (1944).

Sassoon, Siegfried, *Memoirs of an Infantry Officer* (1930).

Schmitt, Bernadotte E., *The Coming of the War*, 2 vols. (1930).

————, *Triple Alliance and Triple Entente* (Berkshire Studies, 1934).

Seton-Watson, Robert W., *Sarajevo, A Study in the Origins of the War* (1936).

Stallings, Laurence, ed., *The First World War: A Photographic History* (1933).

Swain, Joseph W., *Beginning of the Twentieth Century* (1938).

Taylor, A. J. P., *Illustrated History of the First World War* (1964).

Thomson, George M., *The Twelve Days* (1964).

Trotsky, Leon, *The History of the Russian Revolution,* 2 vols. (1932, 1937).

Tschuppik, Karl, *Ludendorff: The Tragedy of a Military Mind* (1932).

Tuchman, Barbara, *The Guns of August* (1962).

Watt, Thomas P., *Dare Call it Treason* (1963).

Wheeler-Bennett, John W., *Brest-Litovsk: The Forgotten Peace* (1939).

———, *Wooden Titan: Hindenburg* (1936).

Wolfe, Bertram D., *Three Who Made a Revolution* (1948).

Wolff, Leon, *In Flanders Fields: The 1917 Campaign* (1958).

Index